Letters to Sala

ARLENE HUTTON is the author of *Last Train to Nibroc*, which received a Drama League Best Play nomination and was a finalist for the Francesca Primus Prize. Regional theatre credits include B Street, Chester Theatre, Cincinnati Playhouse in the Park, Florida Studio Theatre, Kitchen Theatre, Mad Cow, Rubicon, and Washington Stage Guild. Her plays, including *I Dream Before I Take the Stand* and *As It Is in Heaven*, have been presented at the Edinburgh Festival Fringe, off- and off-off-Broadway, in London, and throughout the world. As of 2020, her play *Letters to Sala* has had more than one hundred and fifty productions in thirty-five states and Canada.

An alumna of New Dramatists and member of Ensemble Studio Theatre, Hutton is a three-time winner of the Samuel French Short Play Festival, nine-time finalist for the Heideman Award, and recipient of the John Lippman and Joe A. Callaway awards. She has received commissions and grants from the EST/Sloan Foundation, NYSCA, the South Carolina Arts Commission, and the Big Bridge Theatre Consortium. Residencies include the Australian National Playwrights Conference, Blue Mountain Center, MacDowell, SPACE on Ryder Farm, Winterthur, and Yaddo. Hutton was twice named the Tennessee Williams Fellow at the University of the South and has taught at the College of Charleston and the Sewanee Writers' Conference. She lives in New York City.

Letters to Sala

A PLAY BY

Arlene Hutton

THE OVERLOOK PRESS
New York, NY

This edition first published in the United States in 2022 by
The Overlook Press, an imprint of ABRAMS
195 Broadway, 9th floor
New York, NY 10007
www.overlookpress.com

Abrams books are available at special discounts when purchased in quantity for premiums and promotions as well as fundraising or educational use. Special editions can also be created to specification. For details, contact specialsales@abramsbooks.com or the address above.

Cataloging-in-Publication Data is available from the Library of Congress. A catalogue record for this book is available from the British Library.

Book design and type formatting by Bernard Schleifer
Manufactured in the United States of America
ISBN 978-1-4683-1603-2
eISBN 978-1-68335-711-7

FIRST EDITION
1 3 5 7 9 10 8 6 4 2

for Lawrence Sacharow,
for Ann, Elisabeth, and Caroline
and, especially, for Sala.

Contents

Preface

"Here, I want you to have these."

When my mother, Sala, handed me a box containing her wartime letters, she changed my life. I woke up that morning as a young wife and mother and working professional; I ended that day as a writer and historian.

Sala kept the secrets of those letters for nearly fifty years. She released them with no strings attached, no instructions, no background information. I knew nothing about what happened to her correspondents or why they and the letters were so important to her. On the eve of heart surgery she feared she would not survive, she had simply decided that the time to share them was now.

The letters changed her life, too. They revealed the compelling story of a beautiful young girl, one of millions of Jews who were enslaved in Nazi labor and concentration camps. As the existence of the letters became known, they attracted the attention of historians and journalists as a unique and important wartime archive. They became part of the permanent collection of the New York Public Library. I published my book, *Sala's Gift*, which was translated into six languages. A documentary team began work on a future film. Behind the stone lions of the New York Public Library, some thirty thousand visitors viewed the letters in an exhibition, which was then adapted by Jill Vexler, traveling to dozens of locations throughout the United States and to Poland and Estonia. Sala's story was told around the world on television and radio, in newspapers and online.

And Arlene Hutton wrote this wonderful play, *Letters to Sala*.

A private person, Sala was sometimes bothered that strangers would know things about her. That she had a boyfriend in the camps. That she smoked. That there was a time that she wanted to renounce her religion. But she set aside her discomfiture as a small price to pay for the gift of knowing that through this play, her friends and her family, most of whom were murdered, would not be forgotten. They had no graves, but every performance would tell their story.

There have now been more than one hundred and fifty productions of *Letters to Sala* at high schools, colleges, repertory theatres, and off Broadway. Nothing pleased Sala more than hearing about that growing army of actors and stage managers and teachers. She treasured every note that they sent to her, wore every T-shirt, read every playbill, and watched every video.

Sala did see one full production of the play: opening night at Rollins College in Winter Park, Florida. I arrived a day early and watched the dress rehearsals. That night, I called my husband in tears. How can I make my mother watch this, I wailed. It is too much for her, to see an actor pretending to be her mother, to relive these gut-wrenching scenes of love and loss.

On my husband's advice, I asked her again if she felt ready to see the play. Yes, she insisted, she would be in the audience, as planned.

We sat together in the dark, my mother and father and me.

When the performance ended and the lights came on, I turned to her, overcome with emotion myself, and asked if she was okay.

"Of course, I am okay," she said. "It's only a play."

She always was my best teacher.

Although art is ultimately an imitation of life, *Letters to Sala* is a journey to the past, an experience of empathy rooted in historical truth. In the darkest days of war and genocide and anti-Semitism, Sala honored these letters as precious sparks of humanity and hope that must be shared with another generation.

Thank you for remembering her.

Ann Kirschner, June 2021

Introduction

THE JOURNEY OF HOW *LETTERS TO SALA*
CAME TO BE WRITTEN

In the fall of 2005, when I was the Tennessee Williams Playwriting Fellow at the University of the South in Sewanee, Tennessee, I received a phone call from director Lawrence Sacharow, who had seen my play about Shakers, *As It Is in Heaven*, at 78th Street Theatre Lab four years earlier.

"I have a play for you to write," Larry said. And that was the beginning of a project that would, off and on, be part of the next ten years of my life.

I flew to New York City for a meeting with Larry Sacharow and Ann Kirschner, Sala Garncarz's daughter, and together they told me Sala's amazing story. Larry had the idea to create a multimedia theatre piece for three actresses. I immersed myself in the galleys of Ann's book about her mother's life, *Sala's Gift*.

Larry gave me assignments for specific scenes: "Write the scene at the train station three different ways." He pieced together a theatrical collage with projections of photos, film, and letters, alongside live scenes and readings of the letters, creating a thirty-minute presentation shown at the New York Public Library in March 2006, featuring Marian Seldes, Wendy vanden Heuvel, and Nina Sacharow. The theatrical event and an exhibition curated by Jill Vexler celebrated the donation of Sala's letters to the Dorot Jewish Division of the library.

During the inevitable wine-and-cheese party that followed, Larry told me that originally Peter Brook had discovered Sala's story and had introduced Ann to Larry. (I'm very happy Peter Brook didn't have the time to create his own version.) Larry suggested there was a longer story to tell and we continued working together, emailing back and forth. Susan Claassen, artistic director of the Invisible Theatre in Tucson, heard about the project, which had been mentioned in press releases. She asked to present a workshop of the script in Arizona the following January. But Larry passed away that summer, suddenly and unexpectedly, less than a year after we had started. The last time I saw him was at the hospital, where he gave me notes from his bed.

After Larry died, Ann Kirschner and I spoke on the phone. "I have two questions for you," she said. "One: Can you finish the play? Two: Do you want to finish the play?" I replied, yes, that I can write a play from such rich material. And no, I don't want to finish the play without Larry. I told her that there's a third question: What would Larry want?

Ann and I decided to continue with the project. But I couldn't write Larry's play; I had to find my own play now. I asked Ann what she wanted. "For the story to reach as many people as possible," she replied. I said, "Okay, then I'm going to look at all the speaking roles these three actors have." It turned out there were two dozen different characters, and that's the play I wrote and developed over a number of years.

Somewhere along the journey Eric Nightengale, my longtime *Nibroc Trilogy* collaborator, signed on, directing three very different productions with students at Stagedoor Manor, Rollins College, and, finally, at the College of Charleston.

Dramatists Play Service published the script in 2014, and high schools across the country quickly found the play—a large cast script, with most of the roles for women; a contemporary story with an historical background; no questionable language or content—and produced it. Many schools have embraced diversity in casting and the play has been produced in huge theatres with lovely set designs as well as on small stages with just a couple of tables and some chairs. Ann and I get letters and emails from students, parents, and teachers across the country, like this one Ann received from Bria, a high school student: ". . . it's impossible to refer to the ensemble as 'characters.' After the cast went through the table read, we had a ten-minute discussion about Sala and about how wrong it felt to refer to them as anything other than people. Real people. Admirable people. . . . it would mean the world to me if you could tell your mother that a student in California, all the way across the country, has utmost respect and admiration for her. Please let her know that I was touched so deeply by her story, and I wish I were there to tell her in person." Another teacher wrote to me: "I can honestly say of all the plays and musicals I've directed with young people, this one got the most positive response of any. The audience was so moved by the story. You could hear many noses sniffling and tears, which I expected, but I was also taken by the laughter that happened as well. Sala, Harry, Elfriede, Chaim, Herbert—their scenes all at one point got great chuckles from the audience. Thank you again for a script that has touched my heart and left such an impact on my students. The conversations I heard them have and the connection they feel to the Garncarz family is so very special."

With such a large cast I never thought the play would be produced in New York City, but after readings at New Dramatists and other venues, the F.A.B. Women's wing of The Barrow Group took a chance, and, as a co-production with my own Journey Company, produced it off-off-Broadway, giving me one more chance to revisit and revise the script. It is that version that is published here.

There are many reasons Ann and Eric and I kept this project going for so long, but I think it's mostly because of young people like Bria. In the play Sala says, "I keep them alive by saving the letters," and that's what all of us are doing—the casts of all the various versions of the play in development, along with New York City producer Christine Cirker, supported by Lee Brock of The Barrow Group—with our audiences as witness. As theatre artists we are keeping these people alive by giving them voices and telling their stories. Perhaps the high point of this journey, so far, was the concert reading at the Museum of Jewish Heritage, a presentation, the closest to Larry's original vision, which was especially meaningful to its audience.

I'm grateful to The Overlook Press for this opportunity to revise the play so it reflects what we learned in a professional workshop. There are a number of changes from the acting edition.

One last thing. During the pandemic shutdown I thought a lot about Sala and viewed her story through new eyes. What does it mean to have to stay indoors? How do we know what to believe when rumors are flying and every day brings reports that are worse than the day before? What are our lives like when we are worried about friends and relatives but can't visit them? How do we live when we feel we can't trust each other, when there is so much hatred in our country? Sala's experiences don't seem so distant anymore.

I think back fondly on Seder nights at the Kirschner family's home, sitting next to Sala. I remember talking to Sala after she watched the production at Rollins College. She grabbed my arm, looked into my eyes, and said, "So many memories, so many memories." Although Sala is no longer with us, her life has had meaning to more people than she ever could have imagined. And knowing her and bringing her story to life on the stage has been one of the most meaningful experiences of mine.

Arlene Hutton
New York City
June 2021

Photographs

Above left: Sala's father, Josef Garncarz

Above right: Sala's mother, Chana Garncarz

Left: Young Sala

Top: Blima and Jakob

Above left: Sala, Raizel, and Joey in New York, 1949

Above right: Raizel in Sweden, 1946

Top left: Harry Haubenstock

Top right: Elfriede Pache

Above: Ala Gertner (left) and Sala

Above: Sala (left) with friends from the Schatzlar camp

Right: Chaim Kaufman

Above: Sala and Harry

Left: Sala and Sidney

Above left: Sala in front of Ansbach synagogue, 1946

Above right: Birthday card drawn by friends in the Schatzlar camp and hand-delivered to Sala, March 5, 1944

Opposite: Sala after the war, Fall 1945, Ansbach, Germany. Photographs by Stanley Kirschner.

The postcard shows handwritten text in German script, with the printed "Postkarte" heading, a postage stamp, postmarks, and address written to:

An
Sala Garncarz
F.A. Buhl-sohn
Judenlager 20
Schatzlar
Bei Trautenau
Sudetengau

Above: Postcard from Sala's brother-in-law in the Sosnowiec ghetto to the Schatzlar camp, April 11, 1943. Note the postage stamp and the "Z" for "zensiert," indicating that the card was reviewed by a German censor.

Left: Birthday card, 1944

Spill and Spell box that held Sala's letters after the war

Top: Sala and Ann

Above: Ann, Elisabeth, Sala (middle), Sidney, and Caroline

Letters to Sala

Credits

Letters to Sala received its New York premiere at TBG Theatre on October 2, 2015. Originally conceived by Lawrence Sacharow and based on the book *Sala's Gift* by Ann Kirschner, the play was directed by Eric Nightengale and co-produced by The Journey Company (Beth Lincks, Producing Artistic Director) and FAB Women@TBG (Lee Brock, Executive Director; Christine Cirker, Managing Producer).

Choreography, Molly St. Pierre; Sean Gorski, Set Design; Eric Nightengale, Lighting & Sound Design; Janine McCabe, Costume Design; Michael Wiernicki, Associate Costume Design; Marina Montesanti, Production Stage Manager; Assistant Stage Manager: Anna Just; Pre-production Manager: James Harker.

SALA	Anita Keal
ANN	Alice Jankell
CAROLINE	Laura Kamin
ELISABETH	Kate McGonigle
YOUNG SALA	Britian Seibert
CHANA	Tamara Flannagan
RAIZEK	Lila Donnolo
BLIMA, BELA	Julie Voshell
LAYA DINA	Danielle Sacks
FRYMKA	Jane Elias
ALA GERTNER	Anne Bates
CHAIM KAUFMAN	Andrew Ash
HARRY HAUBENSTOCK	Ben Becher
ELFRIEDE PACHE	Rachel Casparian
HERBERT PACHE	Michael Piotrowski
LUCIA	Missy Hargraves
GLIKA, ZUSI	Colie McClellan
SARA	Danielle Sacks
NAZI OFFICER	Thanos Skouteris
NAZI SOLDIER	Sean Gorski
NAZI GUARDS	Michael Piotrowski, Steven Russo
DANCERS	Julie Voshell, Colie McClellan, Carlota Lopes, Michael Piotrowski, Sean Gorski, Thanos Skouteris
SIDNEY KIRSCHNER	Steven Russo

Characters

(may double, as needed)

New York City:
SALA GARNCARZ, an older woman who survived the Holocaust
ANN, Sala's daughter
ELISABETH, Sala's granddaughter, late teens
CAROLINE, Elisabeth's younger sister, about the same age as
      Young Sala

In Sosnowiec, in the camps, after the liberation:
YOUNG SALA, 16 years old at the beginning of the play

In Sosnowiec:
CHANA, Sala's mother
RAIZEL, Sala's sister
BLIMA, LAYA DINA, Sala's other sisters
GLIKA, Sala's cousin
BELA, FRYMKA, SARA, friends from home

In the camps:
ALA GERTNER, 20s, an elegant woman from a prosperous
      Jewish family
CHAIM KAUFMAN, a friend of the Garncarz family
HARRY HAUBENSTOCK, a handsome prisoner
ELFRIEDE PACHE, a young German woman
HERBERT PACHE, her brother, a Nazi soldier
LUCIA, GUCIA, ZUSI, RACHEL, fellow prisoners in the labor camps
NAZI OFFICER, YOUNG NAZI SOLDIER, NAZI GUARDS

After the liberation:
SIDNEY KIRSCHNER, an American soldier

Setting

New York City, 2004–2005
Poland, Germany, and Czechoslovakia, in the 1940s

Notes on Casting

The play can be performed by as few as five women and one man, but the preferred casting would be at least eight women and three or four men. A school production could be done with a much larger cast, eighteen or even up to thirty or more, as there are twenty-five named speaking roles and the opportunity for an ensemble in the camp scenes.

In a small cast version, the actresses playing ANN, ELISABETH & CAROLINE could double as ALA, RAIZEL, BLIMA, but the actress playing YOUNG SALA should not double. One actor could play all the men, since they never appear onstage together, but the addition of a second actor gives the opportunity for more soldiers. The Nazi dialogue can be trimmed or cut to accommodate the production. Running time is about ninety-five minutes. The playwright encourages the use of nontraditional casting. There were tens of thousands of Africans living in Germany and surrounding nations at the time of the Holocaust, in addition to Roma and other ethnic groups; some of them ended up in the camps.

Visual Elements

There are many ways to stage this play and it has been exciting to see it produced with no scenery or with elaborate scenery; with projections or not; with live music, taped music, or no music; in a large proscenium theatre or a black box or in the round.

Maybe the actors change costumes. Maybe they don't. It is possible that there is a growing pile of clothing, especially coats, that becomes a mountain by the end of the play. There could be a projection screen showing images and indicating dates and place names.

There are three main playing areas that may overlap and intersect:

- A table with chairs, representing New York City in 2004. All the scenes with Ann and Caroline and the older Sala use this playing area.
- Another table and chairs, representing the Garncarz home in Sosnowiec. Letters from Raizel are read from this playing area.
- Nonspecific areas. The rest of the action—the train station, the camps, etc.—takes place center stage or at other locations.

There are no blackouts between scenes. The changes are fluid, with the scenes overlapping and interrupting each other when possible, as the actors switch from the past to the present. We may not even know sometimes if it is then or now, if the story is being acted out or if a memory is being told. The actors in one scene should never freeze while a scene is occurring on another part of the stage, but in the shadows go about their business.

The physical letters themselves are an integral part of the play and should be shown whenever possible. Images of the actual letters and cards may be projected on a screen or wall. Actors reading the letters may hand them to Sala. She might bury them under the mound of clothing or in hiding places on the set, pass them off to her friends or even make members of the audience co-conspirators in her need to hide and keep her mail. Young Sala can see the writers when they are reading, but her eyes follow the letters as they are "mailed."

It is essential that historic photos of the letters and Sala's friends and family be shown to the audience: as projections or in the program or as a lobby display. Sala risked her life to keep these and it is important they be seen. The images may be found online at the website with resources for producing and studying the script.

The play moves back and forth in time and space, from 2004 in New York City to 1940s wartime Poland, Germany, and Czechoslovakia.

There are many ways to stage this play, but all that is really necessary are a couple of tables and some chairs. Perhaps there is scenery. Or not. Perhaps there are projections of dates and places as well as photographs of the people the characters are based on. But there are always three major playing areas: Ann's New York City apartment in 2004, represented by a dining table and three or four chairs; the Garncarz home, a tenement in 1940s Poland, which also has a table and chairs; and a general playing area where all the other scenes take place. This neutral space becomes the train station, a home in Geppersdorf, various areas in several labor camps in Nazi Germany, and places in Europe after the liberation.

Lighting directs the audience's attention from one playing area to another, but there are no blackouts. The action moves fluidly between scenes and there is no gap in the dialogue between scenes; actors should enter a new scene while the previous one is still going on. The life in New York may continue in a dim light during a scene in Poland or the camps. And vice versa.

Act One

NEW YORK CITY, 2004, AND SOSNOWIEC, POLAND, 1940.

Lights up on SALA, *sitting at the table in Ann's apartment.* SALA *holds a child's game "Spill and Spell" box and stares at the scene playing out on the other side of the stage.*

There, representing the Garncarz home, a tenement in 1940s Poland, is another table and three chairs. Lights up on CHANA, *an older Jewish woman, and her daughters* RAIZEL, *a frail-looking young woman with glasses, and* BLIMA. *They are all looking at an official-looking letter. There is a sense of urgency; the lines often overlap.*

ANN *enters with a small suitcase and a file folder, followed by her daughters* ELISABETH *and* CAROLINE, *who carries a card. On the other side of the stage,* YOUNG SALA, *a girl of sixteen, rushes in carrying a small package, as the older* SALA *watches from across time and space.*

The scenes in the past and present happen simultaneously and overlap.

ANN

Entering.
Mother! Mother, it's time to go.

YOUNG SALA

Running in.
Mother! Mother! I found some bread.

RAIZEL

(To BLIMA.*)*
I'll write you every day.

YOUNG SALA

Mother!

BLIMA

(To YOUNG SALA.*)*
Sala, Hush.

CAROLINE

Bubbe! I wrote you a letter to read at the hospital.

ANN

I've got all your paperwork.

YOUNG SALA

Mother!

RAIZEL

Sala, be quiet.

CAROLINE

Here! I'll put it in your suitcase.

ELISABETH

Seeing the box.
Are you going to play "Spill and Spell" at the hospital?

ANN

I haven't seen that game in years. I thought it was lost.

CHANA

Looking at an official-looking letter.
What if the letter had been lost in the mail?

CAROLINE

I want to play.

ELISABETH

(To CAROLINE.*)*
You'll be at summer camp.

YOUNG SALA

Mother, let me go.

RAIZEL

It wasn't lost in the mail. It came. The letter came. It wasn't lost.

ANN

Mother. I'm packing your blue sweater. Your room might be chilly.

CHANA

Looking into the suitcase.
This sweater won't keep you warm.

BLIMA

Take my blue wool.

YOUNG SALA

I could go in your place, Raizel.

RAIZEL

The brown sweater's good enough.

ELISABETH

I'll miss you, Bubbe.

ANN

Is your grandfather ready?

ELISABETH

Poppy's in the car with Dad.

BLIMA

(To YOUNG SALA.*)*
Sala, did you find some bread?

YOUNG SALA
Yes.

BLIMA
Good girl. *(To* RAIZEL.*)* How's your stomach?

ANN
(To SALA.*)*
Mother, I'm packing your medicines. Just in case. They should have it on your chart, but just in case. I'll be with you most of the time, anyway.

ELISABETH
(To SALA.*)*
How long will you be gone?

CAROLINE
(To SALA.*)*
I'll write you letters while I'm gone for the summer.

ANN
(To SALA.*)*
Would you rather have your brown sweater?

CHANA
You translated the letter wrong. Isn't it in German? Maybe you misunderstood.

RAIZEL
No, Mother, I didn't. The letter says that I have to go to the labor camp.

CAROLINE
You'll be here when I get back from the summer, won't you?

BLIMA
(To RAIZEL.*)*
Did you pack your medicine?

CHANA
But you're a teacher. Doesn't it say you're a teacher? Don't they know you're a teacher?

RAIZEL
Mother, the schools are closed.

CHANA
You're not strong. Don't they know you're not strong? Neither you nor Blima are strong.

YOUNG SALA

I'm strong.

RAIZEL

Sala.

BLIMA

Looking in the suitcase.

I can't find your medicine.

RAIZEL

There's none left.

ELISABETH

(To ANN.*)*

How long will Bubbe be in the hospital?

SALA

(To ELISABETH.*)*

That depends.

CAROLINE

On what?

SALA

(Teasing.)

On how hard you pray for me.

ELISABETH

Bubbe!

CAROLINE

(Overlapping.)

Bubbe!

YOUNG SALA

(Calling offstage.)

Poppa!

CHANA

Shush!

BLIMA

He's praying.

SALA

However long God wills me to be in the hospital, that's how long I'll be in the hospital.

ANN

Mother! *(Looking around.)* Where's my jacket?
> ANN *exits.*

ELISABETH

> *(To* SALA.*)*
I'll pray for you.

CAROLINE

I love you, Bubbe.

ELISABETH

I love you, too.

SALA

And I love my granddaughters. My greatest joys. The greatest joys of my life. Don't worry. Don't worry about Bubbe. Whatever happens, it will all turn out fine. You have your mother and your father and your aunts and uncles and your sister. And your Grandpoppa. You have your family.

YOUNG SALA

> *(To* BLIMA.*)*
Blima, I could go.

RAIZEL

> *(To* YOUNG SALA.*)*
You're a child.

BLIMA

> *(To* YOUNG SALA.*)*
No. *(To* RAIZEL.*)* This isn't much bread.

YOUNG SALA

It's all I could find.

BLIMA

> *(To* YOUNG SALA.*)*
Go find some writing paper.

YOUNG SALA

> *(To* RAIZEL.*)*
I could go instead of you.

RAIZEL

The letter has my name on it.

YOUNG SALA *picks up the letter and reads.*

YOUNG SALA

"By order of the Jewish Council of the Elders, Raizel Garncarz will report on October 28, 1940, for six weeks of work at a labor camp . . ."

CHANA

(To RAIZEL.*)*

Do you have enough medicine for six weeks?

YOUNG SALA

I could work in a labor camp.

BLIMA

(To YOUNG SALA.*)*

Find some paper. And pencils.

YOUNG SALA

Let me go in Raizel's place.

CHANA

You're too young.

RAIZEL

The letter came for me.

YOUNG SALA

Will I get a letter?

CHANA

(Quickly.)

No.

BLIMA

(Quickly.)

No.

RAIZEL

(Quickly.)

No.

YOUNG SALA

I could go instead of you.

CHANA

You don't know what you're saying.

YOUNG SALA

You have a better answer?

RAIZEL

Don't speak to your mother like that.

YOUNG SALA

Your stomach gets upset when you travel. I can eat almost anything. *(A beat. No one disagrees with her.)* The letter says they're going to pay.

CHANA

Does it really say that?

BLIMA

Yes.

RAIZEL

The letter says they will pay for the work.

YOUNG SALA

I can work. I can work as well as Raizel can. I can.

(*To* RAIZEL.)

I can work better than you.

(*To* CHANA.)

Nothing else makes sense but for me to go.

CHANA

Nothing makes sense.

RAIZEL

My stomach hurts.

YOUNG SALA

See.

BLIMA

What can we do?

CHANA

We can wait and see what happens.

RAIZEL

No, we can't wait. Each family has to pay a tax. Or send one person to work.

YOUNG SALA

You're sick. You can't go.

BLIMA

If we had money to pay the head tax—

YOUNG SALA

I'm going in your place. It's the only answer.

CHANA

No.

RAIZEL

My head hurts. I can't think.

YOUNG SALA

(Over her shoulder, to a far corner of the room.)

Poppa?

RAIZEL

Don't bother Poppa.

BLIMA

(Overlapping.)

He has enough to worry about.

CHANA

(Overlapping.)

God help us.

A car horn is heard.

ELISABETH

Poppy's waiting in the car.

SALA

Then go keep him company! Go!

CAROLINE

I'll play "Spill and Spell" with you when I come home from camp!

ANN *enters.*

ANN

All set?

ELISABETH

I've got Bubbe's suitcase.

CAROLINE

I'll write you.

The car horn honks again.

SALA

Go on. Your mother and I will be down in a minute.

CAROLINE *and* ELISABETH *exit.*

ANN

Mother, the car's waiting.

SALA *holds out the child's "Spill and Spell" game.*

SALA

You should have these.

ANN

What is it?

SALA

My letters from camp.

ANN

Mother, we have to leave.

SALA

Come here. Sit down. Open the box.

ANN

I don't understand.

SALA

These are my letters from the war.

ANN *opens the box and pulls out a packet of letters.*

This is what I have, this is something I never discussed with you before. I was in a labor camp.

ANN

A labor camp?

SALA

During the war.

ANN

A concentration camp?

SALA

No. A labor camp. What do you want to know?

As ANN *looks through the box of letters,* SALA *stares at the other side of the stage, watching her past, in Poland.*

YOUNG SALA

I'm going.

RAIZEL

One of us has to go.

CHANA

(To RAIZEL.*)*
You can't go.

BLIMA

Then it has to be Sala.

YOUNG SALA

It'll be an adventure.

RAIZEL

I'll write to you.

The lights begin to fade on the Garncarz women as they pre-pare for YOUNG SALA's *departure. If the actors exit the scene, it is with purpose, i.e. carrying off the suitcase or the bread. In New York,* SALA, *watching, is interrupted by* ANN, *who has been looking through the letters.*

ANN

Here's your name.

SALA

What?

ANN

Holding up a letter.
This envelope has your name on it.

SALA

Yes.

ANN

(Reading.)
"Geppersdorf."
          (To SALA.*)*
Where's Geppersdorf?

SALA

(Impatient.)
It was Geppersdorf. A camp.

ANN

A concentration camp?

SALA

No. A labor camp. You don't know anything.

ANN

How should I know about something you never, never mentioned? Not to
me, not to the girls.

SALA

You knew I was in the war.

ANN

Yes, but this is different from any of the stories you've told us.

SALA

So now I tell you.

ANN

There are hundreds of pieces of paper here.

SALA

I never counted.

ANN

Who wrote all these letters?

SALA

My sisters. Friends from Sosnowiec. Friends from camp. Ala. Ala wrote me
for a very long while.

ANN

Who was Ala?

SALA

A friend from the camps.

ANN

"Camps"? More than one?

SALA

Three or four. I don't remember.

ANN

You were in three or four different camps?

SALA

Maybe five?

ANN

Five?

SALA

It was a long time ago.

ANN

You were in five different labor camps.

SALA

No. It was seven.

ANN

Seven!

SALA

Yes. Let's go.

ANN

Wait. How did you save all these letters?

SALA

I hid them.

ANN

I can't wrap my mind around this. How did you get mail? You got letters?
In a camp?

SALA

Yes.

ANN

And you saved them? How did you—

SALA

They were important to me.

ANN

So important you never told me about them? Where are these people now?

SALA

Your Aunt Rose is in Brooklyn.

ANN

Yes, of course. But what happened to the others?

SALA

Most of them didn't survive the war.

(*A beat.*)

I'm tired now. Let's go.

ANN

Okay. We'll look at these later.

SALA

The letters are yours now.

ANN

We can talk about them later. After you come back home from the hospital. Do you have everything?

SALA

I don't need much.

ANN

Mother!

SALA

What?

ANN

Stop worrying.

SALA

Who's worried?

ANN

They do bypass surgery every day. It's a common procedure.

SALA

(*Blowing on her fingers.*)

Puh-puh. Take care of the letters.

Lights change. In half light SALA *watches the next scene, until at some point* ANN *steers her out the door.*

THE TRAIN STATION IN SOSNOWIEC, POLAND. OCTOBER 28, 1940.

On the other side of the stage, YOUNG SALA *and her mother* CHANA *are at the train station in Sosnowiec, Poland. There is much activity among the crowd: suitcases, goodbyes, etc. If lines are needed for guards, they could be "Bleib genau da, wo ich gesagt habe." [Stay where I tell you.] "Name." [Name.] "Geh dahin." [Go there.] "Aus dem Weg." [Out of the way.] The* GUARDS *are stern but not brutal, focused on giving directions.*

CHANA

God help you.

YOUNG SALA

I have to get on the train now.

CHANA *cries.*

Mother, people are watching us. Don't make them notice us. It's bad.

ALA, *a well-dressed woman, walks over to* YOUNG SALA *and* CHANA.

ALA

(To CHANA.*)*
Don't cry.

CHANA

(Crying.)
My daughter . . . my child.

ALA

You're worried.

CHANA

Yes.

ALA

Look at me. Don't worry, don't cry. She's going to be all right, do you understand what I'm telling you? Look at me. Listen to what I'm telling you. It will be all right. Don't worry. Don't cry, she's going to be with me. Your daughter, she'll be all right, I'm going to watch over her all the time. I'll take care of your child.

CHANA

God bless you.

ALA

(To CHANA.*)*
My name is Ala Gertner.

(To YOUNG SALA.*)*
What is your name?

YOUNG SALA

Sala.

ALA

Ala and Sala. Almost the same.

(To CHANA.*)*
Ala and Sala.

CHANA

My little Sala.

ALA

(To CHANA.*)*
There. Don't cry. Ala and Sala. It was meant to be.

A train whistle is heard.

GUARD

(Yelling orders.)
Araus! Araus!

> As YOUNG SALA *and* ALA *exit, lights fade on the train station and come up on the New York City side of the stage. Time has passed.* ANN, ELISABETH, *and* CAROLINE *are at the table showing* SALA *translations of the letters. The lines overlap.*

ANN

The letters are in three different languages.

CAROLINE

Look, Bubbe!

SALA

I don't know if I can read them.

ANN

I've been finding translators.

ELISABETH

Polish, German, Yiddish.

ANN

It's taken all winter.

ELISABETH

Mom's been busy.

ANN

I've had about half the letters translated.

ELISABETH
(*To* SALA.)
The entire time you were in Florida!

CAROLINE

I've been reading the translations.

ANN

I'm working on the rest.

CAROLINE

It's so exciting!

ELISABETH
(*To* SALA.)
And we found something you wrote.

CAROLINE
(*To* ELISABETH.)
Let me tell her!

ELISABETH

I'm the oldest. I get to tell her. There were these pages, like torn out of a diary.

CAROLINE *picks up a piece of paper and holds it out.*

CAROLINE

Look! Look at this!

SALA

(Confirming.)
That's my handwriting.

ANN

It's dated October 28, 1940. The date jumped out at me. That's the date
you went away from home.

SALA

That's my handwriting. But I can't read it.

ELISABETH

You can't read your own handwriting?

SALA

(Pointing.)
That's "father."

ANN

Yes! Here's the translation.

SALA

(Reading.)
"Oh, my dear father, will you miss your Salusia a lot?" *(To her granddaughters.)* See, he called me Salusia. *(Reading.)* "My father cried." *(To
her granddaughters.)* Yes, he did cry when we were saying goodbye. *(Reading.)* "Onwards. We started out. Where to? Why? Only the future will tell."
(She chokes up.) Hard.

ELISABETH

Bubbe.

CAROLINE

Bubbe. We thought you'd be happy.

ANN

(Reading.)
"I tried to keep a smile on my face as best I could, but my eyes were filled
with tears. One must go on bravely and courageously, even if the heart is
breaking."

A LABOR CAMP IN GEPPERSDORF, GERMANY. OCTOBER, 1940.

ALA *and* SALA *are in the camp. There may be guards and other prisoners around.*

ALA

Listen to everything I tell you.

YOUNG SALA

How long will we be here?

ALA

Not long.

YOUNG SALA

Longer than six weeks?

ALA

Perhaps.

YOUNG SALA

The letter said for six weeks.

ALA

Listen to me. Listen to what I tell you. You must do everything they say. Everything, do you hear me? Whenever they ask who is able to do this or that, you say, I am, I can do it. And you learn how to do whatever it is they want you to do. Can you read?

YOUNG SALA

Yes.

ALA

German?

YOUNG SALA

A little.

(A beat.)

I can learn.

ALA

Good girl. Can you type?

YOUNG SALA

No.

(A beat.)

I can learn.

ALA

You don't have time to learn. What can you do?

YOUNG SALA

I don't know.

ALA

Can you cook?

YOUNG SALA

I can boil vegetables.

ALA

Surely your mother taught you how to cook.

YOUNG SALA

I make the fire.

ALA

Can you sew?

YOUNG SALA

Yes.

ALA

Can you sew well?

YOUNG SALA

We take in tailoring at home.

ALA

Good. Maybe they'll let you sew for the officers. That would be good work for you. Always remember that they need us. Show that you're willing to work. That you'll work hard.

YOUNG SALA

If I work hard, will I get to go home sooner?

ALA

Work hard no matter what. You're pretty. You don't look like a Jew. They already like you. Maybe they'll let you mend their clothes. Someone has to. Sewing is a very good skill to have.

YOUNG SALA

Can you sew?

ALA

No, but I can type. I'm a fast typist. And I read and write German, Polish, Yiddish. They'll need me in the office.

YOUNG SALA

I want to work in the office with you.

ALA

Better you sew. I'll tell them you come from a tailor's family. There. That's settled. And I'll make certain we bunk together. I promised your mother I'd take care of you. And that's what I'll do. "Sala" and "Ala." It was meant to be.

> ALA *exits.* YOUNG SALA *pulls out a pencil and paper from her pocket.*

> *Lights change to the New York City side of the stage.* ANN *is working at the table,* ELISABETH *beside her.*

ELISABETH

Everything's different since we got the letters.

ANN

What do you mean?

ELISABETH

This morning. I was at the bus stop with Bubbe. It was cold. I wanted to complain about it, about the cold. I wanted us to take a taxi. But I thought about Bubbe, about how cold Bubbe must've been, in the camps—it must've been really cold there—and so I couldn't say how cold I was at the bus stop. Bubbe never says how cold it was in the camps. But it must've been.

ANN

Yes. It must've been very cold.

ELISABETH

I wanted to take a taxi. But I knew Bubbe wouldn't. She never complains about the cold.

ANN

No, she doesn't.

ELISABETH

Bubbe's getting old.

ANN

Yes.

ELISABETH

When she's gone we'll still have her letters.

Lights up on YOUNG SALA, *writing a postcard.*

YOUNG SALA

Dear Raizel—I arrived at the camp. Lieb is here, cousin Glika's boyfriend, but I haven't been able to speak to him. Men aren't allowed in the women's barracks.

YOUNG SALA *sees a* GUARD *coming and hides the letter in her pocket.*

Lights change to ANN *and* SALA *in New York City; it can be only moments after* ANN's *conversation with* ELISABETH.

ANN

Aunt Rose won't answer any of my questions. I try and try.

SALA

Maybe she doesn't want to talk about it.

ANN

She has to talk about it.

SALA

Why? Why make her remember those times if she doesn't want to?

ANN

She knows things. Horrible things that she won't talk about.

SALA

(With a shrug.)
So? I had it easy.

ANN

I didn't mean that. You're just like Aunt Rose. You don't answer my questions, either!

SALA

I gave you the letters.

ANN

After more than fifty years!

SALA

You wanted them sooner?

ANN

Why didn't you ever tell us about being in the camps?

SALA

You and your brothers were children. I wanted you to be happy. I didn't
want you to live with any guilt because of what I went through. I didn't want
you to hate other people because of what I went through.

ANN

But the letters. Hidden away. Didn't they mean anything to you?

SALA

They meant everything to me. They meant connection with the outside
world, connection with my family, connection with my friends. It was a
feeling that . . . that it's worthwhile fighting . . . and hope . . . and not to give
up . . . that we're going to survive. Because there was always that hope,
that if I was lucky, maybe someone else was lucky. If I'm alive, maybe
somebody else is alive, too.

SOSNOWIEC, POLAND. NOVEMBER 4, 1940.

RAIZEL is seated at her table, writing a letter.

RAIZEL

Dear Sister—We were so happy to get your postcard. But don't think that
we stopped worrying just because we received some mail—because you
don't write much about yourself.

*Through time and space, RAIZEL hands the letter to YOUNG
SALA. [Note that throughout the play, whenever the letters are
handed off, there is no eye contact between the actors, whose
focus is always on the paper itself.]*
(Reading.)
If you possibly can, take the opportunity to learn to type. It can't hurt. If I
get the chance, I'll try to learn typing here, too.

RAIZEL & YOUNG SALA

(Reading / writing.)

Write more—send us details. How's the food? What do you eat? Do you like the food? Do you cook? Where do you sleep? Do you have heat?

YOUNG SALA

(Writing her own letter.)

Dear Sister—I sleep in a bunk with Miss Ala. One of the girls in my barracks brought some cheese, which she shares with us. One morning we had bread and butter. For dinner we have cabbage soup. We work long hours and it's cold here. My thoughts are with you.

RAIZEL & SALA & YOUNG SALA

(Reading.)

Write as often as possible! We're anxious to know everything.

New York City. ANN *is working.* CAROLINE *and* ELISABETH *enter.*

ELISABETH

Bubbe's crying.

ANN

Again?

CAROLINE

It's your fault.

ANN

Mine?

CAROLINE

She never used to cry.

ELISABETH

She cries a lot.

ANN

She's remembering things.

ELISABETH

It's making her cry.

ANN

Sometimes bringing up the past does that.

CAROLINE

You should leave Bubbe alone.

ELISABETH

Every time she's in town you talk about the war.

CAROLINE

You're like interrogating her.

ANN

I'm doing research. I think I'm going to write a book.

CAROLINE

A book about Bubbe?

ANN

A book about the letters. I'm trying to find out what happened to everyone she knew. Everyone who wrote to her. I'm making new discoveries every day. It's exciting.

ELISABETH

She's not letting on, but it makes her sad thinking about it.

ANN

It's good for her. It's good for her to remember. I find out about something in my research, and I ask her about it, and she remembers things she hasn't thought about in over thirty years. It's all going to be in the book.

CAROLINE

You're like a vulture.

ANN

Caroline!

CAROLINE

Interrogating Bubbe until she cries.

(*To* ELISABETH.)

Right?

(*To* ANN.)

Mom, she's an old woman. You can't ask her questions all the time. It's hard on her.

ELISABETH

Why do you tell her everything?

ANN

Well, wouldn't you want to know? If you were Bubbe?

CAROLINE

Maybe she doesn't want to remember everything.

ELISABETH

Have you asked her?

ANN

Wouldn't you want to know what happened to your friends?

CAROLINE

Didn't they all die?

ELISABETH

(To CAROLINE.*)*
She's afraid Bubbe's gonna die before she gets all the answers.

CAROLINE

(To ANN.*)*
Do you care about the letters more than you care about Bubbe?

ELISABETH

What?

CAROLINE

Do you care about the letters more than you care about us?

ANN

Just stop it, you two! These are important documents. These letters have to be researched. Preserved.

CAROLINE

I'm tired of the letters. I want things to be the way they used to be.

ANN

Things can never be the way they used to be.

> *There are whistles and shouts from the other side of the stage,
> as* CAROLINE *stomps off in a huff. With a look to her mother,*
> ELISABETH *follows* CAROLINE. ANN *sighs wearily and keeps
> working.*
>
> *In the Geppersdorf camp* ALA *enters and pulls* YOUNG SALA
> *aside.*

ALA

I saw your letters under the mattress.

YOUNG SALA

You were looking through my things?

ALA

It's hard not to see them when I'm making my bed.

YOUNG SALA

Why are we only allowed to write two letters a week?

ALA

That's the rule. It's not worth getting in trouble over.

YOUNG SALA

My sister gets mad if my friends get a letter and she doesn't.

ALA

We're not allowed to keep mail. Read it and throw it away.

YOUNG SALA

I'll find a better hiding place.

ALA *exits.*

Lights up immediately on ANN *and* SALA. ANN *is reading from* SALA's *journal pages.*

ANN

(Reading.)

"Miss Ala cheers us up every day. She's a terrific and courageous woman. She adjusts to the circumstances without fighting them. What's more, she gives us hope."

(Repeating.)

"She gives us hope."

(To SALA.*)*

Do you remember these diary pages?

SALA

Not at all. I don't remember writing it. I don't remember having it. Maybe when I start reading . . . but I don't remember this. It was so long ago. I have no recollection.

SALA looks to the other side of the stage, ANN continues working, and the lights change.

As YOUNG SALA starts looking for cubbyholes, she is handed mail from her friends back home.

BELA
(Speaking to SALA through time and space.)
Sala! We read the postcard you sent your parents. Why don't you write to us? Bela.

Without looking at her, BELA holds out her letter to YOUNG SALA, who takes it.

SARA
(Speaking to SALA through time and space.)
We miss you! Write to us. Sara.

YOUNG SALA takes the letter from SARA and hands her own letter to FRYMKA.

FRYMKA
Holding SALA's letter.
Sala! Finally a letter from you. It's hard to believe you are so far away from us.

SARA
I hear you left behind a few broken hearts. Write to us.

FRYMKA
There is nothing new here. Write to us!

BELA
Delivering her letter.
Write to us!

SALA
Delivering her letter.
Write to us!

FRYMKA
Thank God all is well. Be strong! *(Delivering her letter.)* Frymka.

BELA, SARA, and FRYMKA have exited. YOUNG SALA begins writing in her diary.

From the New York City set, dimly lit, SALA *has been observ-
ing the previous scene. Lights come up as* CAROLINE *and* ELIS-
ABETH *enter, mid-argument.*

CAROLINE

What would you have done?

ELISABETH

What do you mean?

CAROLINE

What would you do? If I got a letter to go to a camp? If I got a letter to
report to a labor camp, what would you do?

ELISABETH

That's a silly question.

CAROLINE

Would you go in my place?

ELISABETH

Would you go in *my* place?

CAROLINE

What would you do if our family got a letter saying I had to go to a labor
camp?

ELISABETH

You couldn't survive a labor camp.

CAROLINE

I could, too.

ELISABETH

Could not.
        SALA *looks at them [or enters].*

CAROLINE

Bubbe did.

ELISABETH

You can't survive a day without your computer.

CAROLINE

What would you do—

ELISABETH

—or phone—

CAROLINE

—if we got a letter?

SALA

Girls!

> [NOTE: *if* SALA *is not onstage, cut this line.]*

ELISABETH

> *(To* CAROLINE.*)*

It'll never happen.

CAROLINE

> *(To* ELISABETH.*)*

But it did. It did happen. It happened to Bubbe. It's all in the letters.

> *Lights change.*

> YOUNG SALA *is hiding a letter.*

ALA

Sala!

> YOUNG SALA *freezes.* ALA *enters.*

Quickly.

YOUNG SALA

What?

ALA

You've just enough time. Take this note to Bernhard. You know who Bernhard is.

YOUNG SALA

The university student?

ALA

Yes. Take this note to him.

YOUNG SALA

Why?

ALA

Shhhh. Quickly.

YOUNG SALA

Now?

ALA

Stop asking so many questions.

YOUNG SALA

Where? I have to ask that question.

ALA

(Laughing.)

At his barracks. Do this one thing for me, please.

YOUNG SALA

We're not allowed near the men's barracks.

ALA

You won't get caught. You're my Sarenka, fast as a deer. You'll never get caught, Sala. You're like a deer, invisible in the woods.

YOUNG SALA *runs offstage.* ALA *exits.*

RAIZEL *is at her table, writing to* ALA.

RAIZEL

(In a formal manner.)

Dear unknown Miss Ala, you're probably surprised why some total strangers are writing to you. We're very obliged to you and grateful for taking care of and protecting our dear Sala, and we want you to know that we consider you a member of our family. Words can't express our appreciation. Be well and happy together. Raizel Garncarz.

Lights change.

In New York, SALA *and* ANN *are at the table,* CAROLINE *and* ELISABETH *nearby. Perhaps it is still the previous New York scene and* ANN *enters.*

SALA

The letters. The letters. Always about the letters.

ANN

What did you expect, that day, when you gave them to me, what did you expect?

SALA

I was going into the hospital. I didn't want you to find them later. I wanted you to have the letters from me with my blessing. This way, I can tell you what I want, that whatever you do with them is okay.

ELISABETH

We can keep them in a safe-deposit box.

ANN

Like a prison?

SALA

Annie.

ANN

People should have access to them. This is an important collection.

CAROLINE

It's not a collection. It's Bubbe's letters.

ELISABETH

(*To* SALA.)

Did you know she was thinking about giving them away?

SALA

I don't care.

CAROLINE

Tell her you want to keep them.

SALA

I'm tired of them.

CAROLINE

Well, what if *we* want to keep them?

SALA

That's between you and your mother.

> *Lights change.* YOUNG SALA *crouches on the floor, writing her own letter as fast as she can, as* RAIZEL *begins another.*

RAIZEL

Sala! How can you neglect us? It's been a long time since we've heard from you. We're crazy and sleepless from worry. Are you sick? Our dear mother cries all night. So many other people are getting mail, but no letter or even a postcard from you. Don't forget me. I'm the ugly one, but I'm the one who writes you!

> YOUNG SALA *takes* RAIZEL's *letter and hides it in her pocket.*
> CHAIM, *a young prisoner, enters.*

CHAIM

Hello!

(*A beat.*)

Do you remember me?

YOUNG SALA

No.

CHAIM

Chaim. I'm Chaim.

YOUNG SALA

(Not recognizing him.)
I'm sorry.

CHAIM

Chaim Kaufman from Olkusz. I know your cousin, Glika.

YOUNG SALA

Oh. You look different.

CHAIM

I used to be much bigger. They don't feed us very well here. It's nice to
see someone from home.

YOUNG SALA

You'll get us in trouble. You're not supposed to be in the women's section.

CHAIM

No, it's all right. I'm the shoemaker here. In Geppersdorf. I'll keep your
feet warm and dry.

YOUNG SALA

Thank you.

CHAIM

I'm the shoemaker of Geppersdorf.

YOUNG SALA

My shoes are fine.

CHAIM

I've been watching you for days, trying to remember where I know you
from. And today it came to me!

YOUNG SALA

You should go.

CHAIM

I'll keep your feet warm!

YOUNG SALA

Go!

CHAIM

I'll write you from my barracks!

As CHAIM *leaves, lights up on* RAIZEL *and* BLIMA *at their table.* RAIZEL *is writing to* YOUNG SALA *as* BLIMA *looks on.*

RAIZEL
(Quickly and very excitedly, almost breathless.)
Dear Sister—Blima is engaged, actually only a pledge, but it was important enough that I couldn't keep from writing you.

Lights switch to CHAIM, *who is composing his own letter.*

CHAIM
My Salusia—Don't we have the right for a better tomorrow, are we not equal with the whole world? I'm sending this late so you could read it in bed. Good night my dear, happy dreams. Sarenka, this letter is not all that good, but it is from Chaim Kaufman.

CHAIM puts the letter in a shoe and walks past YOUNG SALA, handing the pair of shoes to her with a wink. YOUNG SALA *hides the shoes.*

The scene with RAIZEL *and* BLIMA *continues.*

BLIMA
On Thursday afternoon, I hear from the matchmaker.

RAIZEL
What's going on, we ask her?

BLIMA
The prince has come!

RAIZEL
In the evening, Blima comes in with—

BLIMA
Goldberg.

RAIZEL
"Goldberg," a nice enough fellow. His face was nothing special, just like all men.
(Quickly and very excitedly, almost breathless.)
On Friday, we asked Blima if this meant a pledge, but she didn't want to say yes.

BLIMA

On Sunday morning, the matchmaker comes again, and now the in-laws are asking to meet. Father actually goes there, taking our brother Moshe David with him.

RAIZEL

Sala—We have to tell you the whole story . . .

> *On the other side of the stage,* CHAIM *enters and startles* YOUNG SALA *as she is reading the letter.*

CHAIM

What are you doing?

YOUNG SALA

(*Putting the letter in her pocket.*)

Nothing.

CHAIM

Hiding your letters, aren't you? Always so mischievous.

YOUNG SALA

I'm working.

CHAIM

You're a hard worker. See how much alike we are? I'm a very hard worker myself. You have no idea how many shoes need repair.

YOUNG SALA

My shoes are fine for now.

CHAIM

I'll make you new shoes.

YOUNG SALA

These are fine.

CHAIM

I can bring you cigarettes. Men offer me cigarettes, to repair their shoes. I don't smoke. But I'll bring you cigarettes, if you like.

> CHAIM *exits.*

> SALA *pulls* RAIZEL*'s letter out of her pocket and reads, as* RAIZEL *and* BLIMA *continue their scene.*

RAIZEL

Goldberg's father said, "I ask you for nothing more than one thing: a pledge."

RAIZEL & BLIMA

"I like the bride."

RAIZEL

"The rest is not important, not money, not furniture. I know that if you had more, you would offer it on your own."

CHAIM *enters.*

CHAIM

I have to tell you something. I can no longer hide my feelings. I have fallen in love, a love that is pure, as pure as you are. Can you love me, Sala?

YOUNG SALA

Time will tell.

CHAIM

No. No. I can't accept the expression "time will tell." No, no, time won't show anything anymore. I don't trust time.

YOUNG SALA

That's all I can say for now.

CHAIM

I have a confession, then. I've decided for good or bad that if you let me down I'll finish my life in obscurity and I shall not share my tragedy with anybody.

A GUARD *sees them together.*

GUARD

(*To* CHAIM.)
Was machst du hier? [What are you doing here?] (*If additional words are needed: "Du sollst Schuhe reparieren, Hurensohn!"*) [You should be repairing shoes, you son of a whore.]

With a nod to the GUARD, CHAIM *leaves. The* GUARD *looks at* SALA *and then exits in the opposite direction.*

BLIMA *and* RAIZEL *continue their letter to* YOUNG SALA.

BLIMA

(*Reciting.*)
Imagine, father comes home, mother goes for flour—

RAIZEL

Blima goes for honey cake and our brother-in-law David for a bottle, and in one hour the pledge is given by the groom! Kisses for you from everyone and our best to your friend Ala. Raizel.

BLIMA

And Blima.

YOUNG SALA *pockets the letter from* RAIZEL *and* BLIMA.

Lights up on GLIKA, *who is writing to* YOUNG SALA.

GLIKA

Dear Sala—Greetings from your cousin Glika! Excuse me for not writing German very well. You know, we never learned German, but now we're told you can only receive letters written in German . . . Sala, you ask me whether I know Chaim Kaufman from Olkusz—but why on earth do you want to know that? I can tell you this: He is from a good family. He is a thoroughly decent person and he has a good reputation. I'll write you again to find out if you spoke to him without a chaperone. Glika.

GLIKA *hands* YOUNG SALA *the letter, who begins to hide it, but is suddenly startled by* LUCIA.

LUCIA

Throw it away. (SALA *ignores her.*) I know you got a letter. I was there when they handed out the mail.

YOUNG SALA

It's from my cousin.

LUCIA

I don't care who it's from.

YOUNG SALA

I've never seen you get a letter.

LUCIA

If I did get a letter, I'd read it. And memorize it. And throw it away. That's what you should do.

YOUNG SALA

I'm sorry you don't get any mail.

LUCIA

Don't you understand? If you're caught with mail, we'll all be punished. You've got to obey the rules. It's better for everyone. Read your letter and throw it away.

YOUNG SALA

I can't.

LUCIA

Of course you can. Who do you think you are, putting the entire barracks in danger, just for a few pieces of paper?

YOUNG SALA

It's all I have.

LUCIA

You get packages from your family, too.

YOUNG SALA

A blanket. From my sister. I'm allowed to keep that.

LUCIA

For now. You're very lucky. You have a blanket. You have a boyfriend.

YOUNG SALA

I don't—

LUCIA

I haven't heard from my husband in months. I don't know where he is. I didn't keep his letters, but I know them by heart.

YOUNG SALA

Ala says we shouldn't lose hope.

LUCIA

Ala! If I'm seeing you hide your papers, the guards are seeing you hide them, too. You need to be more careful. And don't take them with you if you're sent to another camp.

YOUNG SALA

I thought we were going to go home soon.

LUCIA

The guards might strip you and search you. And if they find letters or photographs they will beat you.

YOUNG SALA

Maybe my sister can find another blanket to send for you.

A NAZI GUARD *approaches.*

GUARD

Komm mit mir, Jude! [Come with me, Jew!]

Frightened, SALA *says nothing.* LUCIA *keeps her eyes down. The* GUARD *takes* YOUNG SALA *by the arm and pulls her across the stage.*

Komm mit mir! [Come with me!]

THE TOWN OF GEPPERSDORF, GERMANY

ELFRIEDE *stands on the other side of the stage. The* GUARD *pushes* YOUNG SALA *toward her.*

ELFRIEDE

You and I are going to stitch uniforms together. My father is a tailor and we have several sewing machines. I hope you sew quickly. There's a pile of fabric here. I hope you're a fast seamstress.

YOUNG SALA

I'll work as fast as I can.

His job done, the GUARD *exits.* ELFRIEDE *waits to see that he is gone and then turns to* SALA.

ELFRIEDE

Welcome! We're so happy you're here. What's your name?

YOUNG SALA

Sala.

ELFRIEDE

Sala. How beautiful. Can you sew? You must be able to sew or they wouldn't have sent you. Do you speak German?

YOUNG SALA

Yes, I do.

ELFRIEDE

Excellent. I'm Elfriede. Would you like some cake? We're told they feed you very well at the camp, that you have meat every day, so you're probably not hungry, but perhaps you'd like a little cake, something sweet.

YOUNG SALA

Thank you.

ELFRIEDE

Don't they have sewing machines where you are? In the camp? They must not or they wouldn't have sent you here to work at our tailor shop. Imagine, they're paying us for you to be here and sew. We'll have such fun together. I'll do my work and you'll do yours. The time will pass quickly. It's no fun working alone. I'm so happy you're here. Do you miss your family? Of course you must. I miss my brother. Herbert. He's away. Do you have brothers and sisters?

YOUNG SALA

Yes.

ELFRIEDE

And nieces and nephews? You must tell me all about them. What fun. Tell me all about your family.

> ELFRIEDE *leads* YOUNG SALA *offstage.*

> RAIZEL *writes from Sosnowiec.*

RAIZEL

(*Reading.*)

Sala, don't be upset that we haven't sent you a package yet. We'll try to take care of that today. Mother was sick but, thank God, she's well again. Now, Sala, I didn't want to tell you, but we haven't had the money for packages until now. I'm bringing this up to explain why we haven't sent you any food. Please give our regards to the entire Pache family and say thank you on our behalf for how well they take care of you. Otherwise, there's nothing new, we're all well, thank God. Raizel. P.S. Regards to Ala.

> RAIZEL *hands* YOUNG SALA *the letter. Just as* SALA *hides the letter in her pocket, a* GUARD *grabs her.*

GUARD

Komm mit mir! [Come with me!]

Although YOUNG SALA *thinks she's going to get in trouble for hiding her letter, again the* GUARD *brings* SALA *to the Pache home. As before,* ELFRIEDE *stands quietly, until he is gone, leaving the two girls alone.*

ELFRIEDE

What beautiful weather today! It's too lovely to stay inside. Mother's decided that the sewing machines are broken today. What a shame. Poor, poor sewing machines. They need a rest. We've been using them too much. Sala, you stitch so quickly that you've worn out the sewing machine! The machines are broken. Let's walk to town. I'm going to show you our town. Oh! You don't need your star today.

> ELFRIEDE *removes* YOUNG SALA's *armband and takes her on a tour of Geppersdorf.*

Come, come on!

> *[These lines can be added for stage travel time, if necessary: "Over there is the castle and the palace. We'll see them another day. The castle goes all the way back to the thirteen hundreds. Can you see the top of the castle? Come on! This way!"]*

Here's our town square. It's so beautiful, isn't it? Don't be shy. Come look. No matter which way you look, so beautiful. Look over there. See that bakery? That's my favorite. Oh! And the church. So old. Some afternoons you can hear the organ. Maybe we'll be lucky today.

YOUNG SALA

We should go back. We've been gone too long.

ELFRIEDE

We just got here. It's such a beautiful day. I'll show you the church and then we'll go to the bakery and get ourselves some treats. We'll sit on the steps of the church and eat them. What fun. It's my favorite thing to do on a nice day, to sit on the steps of the church and eat a cake while the organ music is playing. Oh! And here's another surprise. We have a doll to send to your niece. A beautiful doll. For your niece. What fun. Should we post the doll to your niece today? No! I'll take it to her myself. Yes. Next week.

> ELFRIEDE *leads* YOUNG SALA *off, as the lights change. On their way, perhaps she hands off to* RAIZEL *the package with the doll inside.*

Lights up on CHAIM, *reading the letter he is writing.*

CHAIM

(Writing.)

Dear Sala—They are moving me to another camp. Sometimes I think about all the things I've lost, but then I remember you, my Sala, my little enchantress, and my heart feels lighter right away, so much lighter! And then I see myself as happy as I have never seen myself before. Chaim Kaufman.

> CHAIM *hands* YOUNG SALA *his letter. While she is hiding it, there is the sound of a whistle. A* GUARD *indicates that* CHAIM *is to go and he exits. When* SALA *turns around,* CHAIM *is gone and the* GUARD *is standing there in his place.*

> As YOUNG SALA *puts the letter in her pocket,* ALA *enters, purposefully.*

ALA

You have to be more careful.

YOUNG SALA

I didn't do anything.

ALA

You went into town.

YOUNG SALA

Elfriede was with me.

ALA

She's a young fool. You have to work hard, very hard, let them see how hard you work, work harder than anyone else. You can never let up, never, do you hear me? It's the only way they'll respect you. They need us. Someone has to do all the work, so they need us. Make certain they know that you are the best worker. Do you hear me?

YOUNG SALA

Yes. I hear you.

ALA

Good.

YOUNG SALA

You tell me to be careful. But you aren't careful. You sneak Bernhard into the barracks, you miss the lineup to meet him, you call out to him during food distribution. So why shouldn't I go to town with Elfriede if I want to?

ALA

You could get put on a transport to goodness knows where.

YOUNG SALA

Chaim is being transferred.

ALA

We'd better get new shoes before he goes.

YOUNG SALA

He said I should try to join him.

ALA

And what would that accomplish?

YOUNG SALA

We'd be together.

ALA

Is that what you want?

YOUNG SALA

His family knows my family.

ALA

So you're going to jump on a transport to be with him, not knowing where you're going. It'll be worse than here, you can count on it. What's so bad? We have friends, work, food. Things'll get worse before they get better and at least here you know what's what. You want to start over at another camp? Listen to me.

YOUNG SALA

I'm listening.

ALA

I can tell when you're paying attention and when you aren't. Listen. You have food here. You have work. You have friends. You want to dig ditches at another camp? Here you are a seamstress. What's so bad about that?

YOUNG SALA

Chaim says—

ALA

Chaim is a good shoemaker. That's all. If you want advice from a shoemaker, ask him about shoes.

(A beat.)

So. That's settled. You received a letter from your family.

YOUNG SALA

Yes. I did.

ALA

You didn't show it to me. What does it say?

YOUNG SALA

Nothing. They're well.

ALA

Did you hide the letter yet?

YOUNG SALA

I haven't had the chance.

ALA

It's still in your pocket?

YOUNG SALA

Yes.

ALA

Read it to me. Read me news from Sosnowiec.

YOUNG SALA

It's nothing, really.

ALA

Why are you being so mysterious? You and I have no secrets. Read the letter.

YOUNG SALA pulls out the letter.

YOUNG SALA

(Reading.)

"We had a visitor who told us about you and Ala, that she is everything for you in that strange place, and that means so much to us."

ALA

Aha! The letter mentions me. Now why didn't you want me to hear that? Read the rest of it.

YOUNG SALA

(Reading.)
"So, on behalf of our dear mother, be obedient, don't do anything to upset her, show your appreciation, because it's very bad when one is forced to be away from one's home, unprotected and far from all that is familiar. So hold on to Ala: she's a treasure. Listen to her. Don't do anything to aggravate her."

ALA

(With a kind smile.)
Your sister is very wise.

YOUNG SALA

Yes, she is.

ALA

Ah, my little Salusia.

> CAROLINE *and* ELISABETH *are on the New York City side of the stage.* ANN *enters, dressed as if she has just come from a meeting, carrying folders.*

ANN

The New York Public Library wants the letters.

CAROLINE

So?

ELISABETH

I thought you wanted some of them to go to a Jewish museum.

ANN

It's the Dorot Jewish Division of the Library. The collection will be available to a broader audience.

ELISABETH

Okay. Are you telling us or asking our opinion?

CAROLINE

She's telling us.

ANN

The Chairman of the Board is very excited—

CAROLINE

—You already talked to—

ANN

They want to do an exhibition—

ELISABETH

A what?

ANN

An exhibition. In conjunction with the donation. And a big opening—

CAROLINE

A party?

ANN

A benefit. In March. The Board needs a decision immediately. There's an opening in their schedule. For an exhibition. The letters will be on view to the public. Aren't you excited?

ELISABETH

It's kind of a surprise, Mom.

CAROLINE

(Angrily.)

So you're just giving the letters away. Permanently?

ANN

That's what a donation means.

CAROLINE

Don't patronize me.

ANN

I'm simply explaining. I'll be happy to talk to you about it when you're rational.

ELISABETH

Calm down, you two.

ANN

I'm calm.

ELISABETH

Let's discuss this.

CAROLINE

This is important.

ELISABETH

All the more reason to be calm.

CAROLINE

She's giving the letters away!

ELISABETH

(To CAROLINE.*)*

Just some of them.

(To ANN.*)*

Right? We're keeping most of them.

ANN

The Library wants the entire collection.

ELISABETH

What?

CAROLINE

But how do they know what the entire collection is?

ANN

There's a list.

CAROLINE

You made a list of all the letters and just said, here, take them!

ANN

It's a collection. Each of the letters is part of the whole story.

ELISABETH

So we don't keep any of them? Not one?

CAROLINE

You're signing them away.

ANN

Donating them. We have digital copies. You each have hard copies. Bubbe has hard copies.

CAROLINE

Copies.

ANN

You can't even read the originals. You have the translations. The words are all there.

CAROLINE

It's not the same.

ANN

Trust me. You don't want the responsibility. What if something should happen?

CAROLINE

What could happen?

ANN

A fire in our building, a water leak from the apartment above us. Anything. The sooner the letters are stored properly, the better.

CAROLINE

They've been safe for fifty years.

ANN

Aren't we lucky! At any time anything could have happened. And now we have this great opportunity.

CAROLINE

It sounds like you've already made up our minds.

ANN

Well, legally, it's up to me. Bubbe gave me the letters.

ELISABETH

Is this what Bubbe wants?

ANN

I told the Board I'd get back to them tomorrow.

CAROLINE

Without a family discussion?

ELISABETH

Mom, how can you make decisions for my children and for Caroline's children, and for our children's children?

ANN

You want to split up the collection? When I'm gone? Half with you and half with Caroline? And then

(*Pointing to* ELISABETH.)

your daughters get some and

(*Pointing to* CAROLINE.)

your daughters get some and where will the letters be fifty years from now? You think some of them won't be lost along the way? They belong in a museum or library and now we have this wonderful opportunity to save them. We have to let the Board know as soon as possible.

CAROLINE

(*Mocking.*)

We?

ELISABETH

This is really short notice.

CAROLINE

We'll discuss it and get back to you.

ANN

The letters need to be someplace where they are protected. Someplace where people can see them.

CAROLINE

They're private.

ANN

They're important historical documents.

CAROLINE

It's family letters and birthday cards.

CAROLINE *stomps off,* ELISABETH *behind her.* ANN *sighs and goes back to the letters.*

Lights up on SARA, *who is reciting her letter.*

SARA

Dear Sala—Your friends back home wonder about what you're doing, what you're thinking. It isn't the same as when you were here. We work from morning until night, and we come home very tired, we ask only that we get through the day and that we'll all see each other and be happy. I believe that with God's help it'll happen, only we mustn't lose hope, we must keep on, keep on, and still keep on. Have you heard about my engagement? I'd love to have you at my wedding! Maybe you'll be able to come back by then. Your friend, Sara.

Lights change.

YOUNG SALA *is back at* ELFRIEDE's.

ELFRIEDE

Your last day with us. How sad. We'll miss you. Will you miss us, Sala? But my mother and I will visit you. How sad that the camp has their own sewing machines now. Who will fix them if they break? Do they have enough needles?

YOUNG SALA

I don't know.

ELFRIEDE

Oh! No, that's me that breaks the needles. Sala, have you ever broken even one needle?

YOUNG SALA

I'm more careful than you are.

ELFRIEDE

Who'll fix my mistakes now? I'll miss you. I will miss you, Sala. I'll be lonely without you. We haven't heard from my brother. We don't know when he'll be home. I wanted to take you to town again. The bakery's closed now, but the organist still plays at the church. We'll visit you, Sala, my mother and me. And bring you a treat.

ELFRIEDE *exits*.

On the other side of the stage, RAIZEL *writes.*

RAIZEL

Dear Sala—May God always look after you. It seems that He has turned away from us here. We imagined a different world, but now we've come to the holiest days of the year and how can one have such angry thoughts? Our dear parents ask you to observe Yom Kippur. Raizel.

RAIZEL *hands the letter to* YOUNG SALA, *who puts it in her pocket.*

On the other side of the stage, in New York City, lights up on CAROLINE *with a laptop computer, about to send an email.* ANN *walks in. This is a heated conversation that gets more intense as it goes on.*

ANN

Talk to me. Tell me. Why do you want to keep the letters?

CAROLINE

Bubbe passed them on to you and you pass them on to us. It's about tradition.

ANN

When has tradition ever mattered to you?

CAROLINE

It matters.

ANN

You roll your eyes at our seder. When we read the Haggadah. When we eat the bitter herbs.

CAROLINE

Mom. I acted like that when I was ten years old.

ANN

You acted like that this last Passover. You complained it was taking too long.

CAROLINE

I cried this Passover. Seeing Bubbe sing the songs.

ANN

Okay. You rolled your eyes the one before.

CAROLINE

That was over a year ago. Maybe I get it now.

ANN

What do you get?

CAROLINE

History. Tradition. That's why we should keep the letters.

ANN

That's why everyone should see the letters.

ANN *exits.*

YOUNG SALA *turns and sees* ALA *packing.*

YOUNG SALA

You're leaving?

ALA

I've been reassigned.

YOUNG SALA

Have I been reassigned, too?

ALA

No.

YOUNG SALA *is silent.*

There are more things I can do from the outside. I can work on getting you released.

YOUNG SALA

You can't leave me.

ALA

The papers are already signed. I'll be living in the Bedzin ghetto, not far from Sosnowiec.

YOUNG SALA

How long have you known?

ALA

Listen to me.

YOUNG SALA

Why should I? You're leaving.

ALA

Listen. Be obedient and well behaved. Keep clean. And work hard. Always work hard. Do whatever they tell you.

YOUNG SALA

I know all that.

ALA

You aren't careful.

YOUNG SALA

I'm invisible, remember?

ALA

You've been lucky. And I've looked out for you.

YOUNG SALA

I don't need you anymore. I'm grown up. I can take care of myself. I don't need anyone to look out for me.

ALA

Good, then.

YOUNG SALA

Go.

ALA

I'm going.

ALA *starts to leave.*

YOUNG SALA

No! No!

ALA

My little Sarenka.

YOUNG SALA

Don't leave me here alone.

ALA

I have to.

YOUNG SALA

Why can't you take me with you?

ALA

I tried—

YOUNG SALA

You didn't try hard enough.

ALA

I'm so sorry. Look at me. You have no idea how angry I am that you have to suffer so much. It's not your fault. Look at me. Don't lose hope.

YOUNG SALA

When will I see you again?

ALA

I'll write you.

RAIZEL *writes a letter from her side of the stage.*

RAIZEL

Dear sister—There's no work. Everything is chaos. We don't know what's going on. Bela Kohn's brother and father are dead. They were hanged in the town square.

(*A beat.*)

My heart is bleeding, because we didn't send you matzo for Passover. Oh, God! Can you believe this? The tablecloth is on the table, the candles are lit, but there's nothing to eat. No matzo. Nothing! I'd rather not write you all that much, just let me say, be happy, happy.

> RAIZEL *walks over to hand the letter to* YOUNG SALA, *as she keeps reading.*

Laugh as much as you can, keep on laughing. Don't worry about us. Have a good time, Sala. Have a good time!

> *As* RAIZEL *"sends" the letter,* TWO NAZI SOLDIERS *enter the room in Sosnowiec.* RAIZEL, BLIMA, *and* CHINA *freeze in fear.*

SOLDIER ONE
Verschwinden! Verschwinden! [Back! Back!]

SOLDIER TWO
Aus dem Weg! [Out of the way!]

> *Other phrases, as needed: "Stehen bleiben." [Don't move.] "Suchen." [Search.]*

> RAIZEL, BLIMA, *and* CHINA *back away. The* SOLDIERS *roughly grab the cloth off the table and kick the table and chairs over.*

> *On the other side of the stage, in New York City, lights up on* CAROLINE *with her laptop computer, about to send an e-mail.*

CAROLINE
(Reading the e-mail she has written.)
Dear Mom—Regardless of what Bubbe has said, I believe she would recognize the significance and severity of this situation. I do not believe she would want her letters to become cold, dead historical documents, rather than living, breathing relics of her family, our family, and generations to come. I urge you to reconsider your position, because if you don't, I'm going to go to the Library Board myself and tell them that you don't have the right to make all the decisions. I am very sorry to do this to you and I do not mean to undermine your project. However, this issue is larger than you and it is larger than me. What you do now will greatly affect our future. Please reconsider your deal with the Library and ensure that the letters remain both a part of history and a part of Bubbe's life.

CAROLINE *presses a key on her computer.*

"Send."

*If there is going to be an intermission, this is where it happens.
Or there could be an interlude with projections of the letters.*

END OF ACT ONE

Act Two

GEPPERSDORF LABOR CAMP. JUNE, 1942.

A man in a Nazi uniform appears, holding a package. YOUNG
SALA *walks up to him as if summoned.*

HERBERT

Are you Sala?

Frightened, YOUNG SALA *nods.*

Sala Garncarz?

YOUNG SALA *nods again.*

You worked for the Pache family?

YOUNG SALA *nods.*

Can't you speak?

YOUNG SALA
(In a whisper.)

Yes.

HERBERT

Yes, what?

YOUNG SALA

Yes, sir.

HERBERT

Yes, you can speak, or yes, you worked for the Pache family?

YOUNG SALA

Yes.

HERBERT

Yes, what?

YOUNG SALA

Yes, I worked for—

HERBERT
(Pointing to writing on the package.)

Is this your name, written here on this package?

SALA *nods.*

Speak. Is this package addressed to you?

> YOUNG SALA

Yes.

> HERBERT

So you're the Sala who worked for the Pache family and this package is addressed to you.

> YOUNG SALA

Yes.

> HERBERT

My parents send their best.

> YOUNG SALA

What?

> HERBERT

My sister Elfriede misses you.

> YOUNG SALA

Elfriede.

> HERBERT

Didn't the guards tell you? I'm Herbert Pache.

> YOUNG SALA

Oh!

> HERBERT

My parents asked, my sister Elfriede demanded that I come see you. They were turned away at the gate. Last week.

He points to the package.

Don't worry. The bread is fresh. Elfriede baked everything all over again. She said to tell you the bakery is still closed, so she baked bread for you herself. She and my mother were turned away and told that you'd been moved. That everyone was moving to a different camp.

> YOUNG SALA

Are we moving?

> HERBERT

I believe so.

YOUNG SALA

Where are they taking us?

HERBERT

I'll try to find out and tell my sister. She talks about you all the time. Well, she talks all the time and sometimes she mentions you.

YOUNG SALA

I miss her.

HERBERT

She wants to know if you are well.

YOUNG SALA

Yes.

HERBERT

(Trying to make a joke.)
Yes, she wants to know, or yes, you are well?

YOUNG SALA

Yes. I am well.

(A pause.)

HERBERT

And your family?

YOUNG SALA *doesn't answer.*

Do you hear from your family?

YOUNG SALA

My family?

HERBERT

My mother told me to ask about your family. You have a little niece. She has a doll.

YOUNG SALA

Yes.

HERBERT

Yes, your niece has a doll, or yes, you hear from your family?

YOUNG SALA

Yes. To both.

HERBERT

Your family. They are . . . all of them . . . still . . . working? All of them?
They are well?

YOUNG SALA

My father was ill but now he's better.

HERBERT

My mother will be happy to hear that your family is well.

A pause. A GUARD *is seen or heard.*

It's time for me to leave.

YOUNG SALA

Please—

HERBERT

I'm sorry.

YOUNG SALA

Don't go yet.

HERBERT

I'm sorry.

YOUNG SALA

Give my best to your family.

HERBERT

My mother and sister will be so happy you are well.

YOUNG SALA

Thank them for the package.

HERBERT

Yes. The move to the other camp will be soon. Did you know that?

YOUNG SALA

No.

HERBERT

Well, then. It's good that there's work. Yes. Goodbye.

HERBERT *exits.*

NEUSALZ LABOR CAMP, POLAND. AUGUST 25, 1942.

> RAIZEL *writes from another part of the stage, or near the Sos-*
> *nowiec area, where the furniture is still turned over.*

RAIZEL

(Reading.)

Dear Sala—We were all taken away! Did you wonder about this new
return address from a camp? That's what happened. They took us away.
We're in a camp near Neusalz. There are many of us from home, all
here together.

> *Still speaking,* RAIZEL *starts to hand* YOUNG SALA *the letter. A*
> GUARD *intercepts the letter, reads it and hands it to* YOUNG
> SALA, *as* RAIZEL *keeps reading.*

(Reciting.)

Don't worry about us. Our sister Laya Dina and her husband apparently
went back home.

> *The* GUARD *moves on.*

On the last day, on August nineteenth, we saw Laya Dina on the way to the
station, which made us feel a little better. But we didn't see our parents.
We don't know where they are!

RAIZEL & YOUNG SALA

(Simultaneously.)

We're worried about our precious, precious parents.

RAIZEL

I'm sending you the photographs of our dear mother and father. We don't
know what happened to them. Have you heard anything about our parents? May God give us some good news. May they be well. Raizel.

Lights change.

YOUNG SALA *writes.*

YOUNG SALA

Dear Diary—No one is getting my letters, so I'm writing to you. The world
is moaning, life is terrible, and there is much to lament. Is it any surprise
that I'm seeing people's misfortune, their sufferings and the injustices
done to them? The world is complaining, and there is a void around us.

Now the winds are blowing hard; what are you bringing us? Will it be fair weather or foul weather? Will there be quiet or turmoil?

> *A train whistle. Shouts from the guards. Women enter and line up for inspection, their backs to the audience. Behind her back,* YOUNG SALA *passes her wallet to the girl beside her and it goes down the line and back, each girl passing it to the one next to her, behind their backs. The* GUARD *inspects the women, never seeing the moving wallet.*

> *The women march off, one of them passing* YOUNG SALA's *letters back to her as they go.*

GROSS PANIOW LABOR CAMP, POLAND. OCTOBER, 1942.

> YOUNG SALA *stands alone, looking around the new camp.*

> HARRY, *a prisoner with privileges and confidence, approaches* YOUNG SALA.

HARRY

I saw you hiding something.

> *(A beat.)*

You're very clever.

> *(A beat.)*

Is it food? No, don't worry. No, you don't have to share your food with me. Keep it for yourself. I won't say anything. But you are definitely the most interesting person here at the camp. What's your name?

YOUNG SALA

Sala.

HARRY

And I'm Harry Haubenstock.

YOUNG SALA

I should get back to my barracks.

HARRY

I'm glad you're here. Hey! I'll write you every day.

YOUNG SALA

Don't get caught.

HARRY

I'll write you every day. From my barracks to yours. What do you think of that? What do you think of me? Do you think I'm too old for you?

YOUNG SALA

I don't know.

HARRY

I'll write you.

> *Like a magician,* HARRY *pulls a folded letter out of the air and hides it in one of* YOUNG SALA's *hiding places. He exits.*

> BELA *and* LAYA DINA *write from the Sosnowiec side of the stage.*

BELA

Dear Sala,

LAYA DINA

My dear sister Sala.

BELA

Your sister Laya Dina is still home with her husband David and all the children.

LAYA DINA

Our children and David are fine but it's been a really bad time. Everyone's been ordered to go, small, grey, old and young, the poor and the rich.

BELA

But your other sisters are with Frymka and they are all being sent to a camp.

LAYA DINA

Our parents and our two sisters, Blima and Raizel, have gone to a work camp together. To Neusalz. Don't worry. They're not alone and you're not alone either. Many, many people are with them. Stay well. Laya Dina.

BELA

Dear Sala—please don't cry! Don't cry. Crying won't help you. Regards, Bela.

> BELA *and* LAYA DINA *disappear.*

YOUNG SALA *is surprised by the sudden entrance of* HARRY,
who has perhaps been hiding nearby.

HARRY

I write you every day.

YOUNG SALA

Careful you don't get caught.

HARRY

The guards like me. I have privileges.

YOUNG SALA

Be careful.

HARRY

I have something for you!

YOUNG SALA

For me?

HARRY

Yes.

As if doing a magic act HARRY *pulls out a cigarette.*

For you! For cute little Sala! I have a half dozen cigarettes and I'll give one
to you. Shall we smoke it together?

YOUNG SALA

Looking around.

I'll save it for later.

HARRY

Cautious little Sala. Don't get caught with it. And don't share it with the
women in your bunk. It's for you only.

YOUNG SALA

Thank you.

HARRY

I think you're the prettiest girl in the camp.

YOUNG SALA

Thank you.

HARRY

What do you think of me?

YOUNG SALA

I think you look like a gypsy.

HARRY

Ha! I'll carry you away to my gypsy wagon. You'll be my little bride.

YOUNG SALA

Don't get caught.

HARRY

I'm a gypsy. We can make ourselves invisible.

He starts to walk off, with a flourish.

Only you will be able to see me.

ALA *interrupts with a letter.*

ALA

(Reading.)

Sarenka, please send me a certificate right away, saying that you worked in Geppersdorf, and specify the dates. Have it signed by the senior officer. I'm trying to get you transferred to where I am. Please tell Harry I hope he's worthy of being loved by my little sweet friend.

YOUNG SALA *looks back toward* HARRY, *but he has disappeared.*

My only wish now? To be together with you both as soon as possible! Salusia, stay well for me and happy with your dear Harry. Remember that love is the most beautiful light in life. We don't need anything else in the world, except, of course, an end to the war.

ALA *hands* YOUNG SALA *the letter. She starts to hide it, as* LUCIA *enters.*

LUCIA

I brought you a potato.

YOUNG SALA

Thank you.

LUCIA

I sewed pockets into my underwear. I can hide potatoes in the pockets. *(She points to the letter.)* You got a letter from your sister?

YOUNG SALA

It's from Ala. She's trying to get me transferred.

> LUCIA

Be careful. You don't know her as well as you think you do.

> YOUNG SALA

What do you mean?

> LUCIA

Be careful.

> LUCIA *exits.* YOUNG SALA *starts to hide her letter, as* HARRY
> *appears.*

> HARRY

You haven't written me in days.

> YOUNG SALA

It's hard. I don't know who to trust anymore.

> HARRY

I was worried.

> YOUNG SALA

I'm fine.

> HARRY

I was on duty from ten to twelve. I kept passing by your window but I couldn't come in.

> YOUNG SALA

I saw you walk past.

> HARRY

I only have a minute.

> YOUNG SALA

I know.

> HARRY

I miss you. I think about you all the time. I'll write you tonight. Tell me you miss me. Do you miss me?

> YOUNG SALA

Yes.

> HARRY

Look at you. So cute. You're so cute. I'd like to hold you in my arms forever. Would that make you happy?

YOUNG SALA

Yes, of course.

HARRY

We've been robbed of our freedom. It's not fair. Oh, this is torture. I should get back.

YOUNG SALA

Don't get caught.

HARRY

How can I leave you? If we were free, I wouldn't leave you alone for even ten minutes. I feel like I belong to you. As if we were married. You're my little bride. And what am I?

YOUNG SALA

You're my gypsy.

HARRY

You're so cute. We'll have our photo taken. Together. Sala and her gypsy.

YOUNG SALA

It's time for me to get back.

HARRY

I have a premonition. I believe that we'll be liberated soon.

As HARRY *exits,* SARA *appears with a letter.*

SARA

Dear Sala—Surprise! Your two sisters are here at my camp. Don't worry about them, we are all in the same room and I'll look after them. I know all about life in the camps, you know. They have very nice work, very light and clean. With me, everything is as always. Write me. Kisses, Sara Czarka.

Overlapping, FRYMKA *chimes in.*

FRYMKA

Dear Sala—I also think of you always, don't worry, your sisters are with us here. Kisses, Frymka Rabinowicz.

FRYMKA *and* SARA *disappear.*

On the other side of the stage, lights come up on SALA *pulling letters from their hiding places and stuffing them into her leather wallet.* HARRY *hands* YOUNG SALA *his own letter, startling her.*

HARRY

Were you afraid yesterday during bunk inspection?

YOUNG SALA

I didn't expect to see you.

HARRY

You should always have a coat ready to throw on.

YOUNG SALA

I loaned it—

HARRY

You looked cute in your pajamas. Here's a cigarette for you.

YOUNG SALA

Thank you.

HARRY

My sweetie, listen carefully. I have some news. The transports are about to be put together. They're moving the men, the road crew.

YOUNG SALA

When?

HARRY

Any day. You should always have your coat ready.

YOUNG SALA

Why?

HARRY

You could volunteer. You could ask if it were possible for you to come along. Maybe they'll need women to work, too. I don't know.

YOUNG SALA

Where are they going?

HARRY

Closer to the road construction. This stretch of the road, it's nearly finished. They're building more camps. To continue the roadwork. When the move comes we can volunteer for the same camp. You have to have your coat ready.

YOUNG SALA

Maybe you can stay here.

HARRY

Say it.

YOUNG SALA

My gypsy.

HARRY

You're so cute. I have a surprise for you. Quick, here in the doorway. Joseph has promised to take our picture.

(To an offstage "Joseph.")

Now. Take the photo.

HARRY *puts his arm around* YOUNG SALA. *They pose for the picture and there is a flash.* HARRY *keeps his arm around her.*

Do you love me?

YOUNG SALA

Yes.

HARRY

How much do you love me?

YOUNG SALA

I love you.

HARRY

What would you give up for me?

YOUNG SALA

What do you mean?

HARRY

Do you love me enough to let me go? To give me complete freedom?

(A beat.)

YOUNG SALA

Yes.

HARRY

You know what this shows? This shows that you love me and only me. You make me very happy. If we were free, I'd make up for what we're missing here.

YOUNG SALA

Can't we stay together?

HARRY

Have your coat ready. I'll see what I can do.

> HARRY *disappears.* YOUNG SALA *races around, grabbing her letters from all their hiding places and stuffing them in her pockets and her leather wallet as there is a lineup to move to another camp.*

> *Train whistles.* GUARDS *shouting, herding the women and men. Perhaps there are groups coming and going. If so, we might hear some lines from the prisoners:* "Have you heard from my brother, Abram?" "What's the word from Sosnowiec?" "What do you know?" "Who have you seen?" "Where have you been?" "Don't lose hope!" "Volunteer for cotton. It's clean work." "The war will be over soon." "Do you know Lieb, from Olkusz?" "Do you know Rabbi Hilberg? Tell him Chancia was transferred." "Remember, there is a God."

BLECHHAMMER LABOR CAMP. OCTOBER, 1942.

> *The* PRISONERS *and* GUARDS *have moved on, revealing* YOUNG SALA *and* HARRY.

HARRY

I'm so sorry. You should've stayed at the other camp. I shouldn't have pressured you to volunteer to leave.

YOUNG SALA

It's very difficult here. I'm hungry.

HARRY

Blechhammer. "Blech." The name sounds like a cat coughing.

YOUNG SALA

Harry.

HARRY

I've made you laugh. Even here I can make you laugh.

YOUNG SALA

I can't stay right now.

HARRY

Same little Salusia. "I can't stay." "I have to go." Write to me.

YOUNG SALA

It's difficult. Someone's always watching.

HARRY

Say it.

YOUNG SALA

I don't feel like it.

HARRY

Say it.

YOUNG SALA

I'm hungry. I don't feel like saying anything.

HARRY

Feed my soul, then. Say it.

YOUNG SALA

My gypsy.

HARRY

So cute.

A NAZI GUARD *appears.*

YOUNG SALA

I don't know if I can get away again. It's too dangerous.

HARRY

You're not afraid of anything. You're always hiding your letters. What if you were caught? Those are just letters. Much better to save up your risks to spend time with me.

YOUNG SALA

You should go.

HARRY

Quickly. A plan. If we get separated . . . write me. Write me as often as you can. And we'll meet later. No matter what happens. No matter how long it takes. In Prague. When this is all over we'll meet in Prague.

GUARD

(To SALA.*)*

Bereit dich vor! [Prepare yourself!]

> *The* NAZI GUARD *escorts* HARRY *off.* SALA *runs around, gathering her letters from their hiding places.*

NEUSALZ LABOR CAMP, POLAND. JULY 24, 1943.

> RAIZEL *and* BLIMA *write from their camp.*

RAIZEL

Sala, why don't you write? We're not getting any mail from dear Laya Dina either. Have you gotten a package from her? How's your work? Your health? We're well, thank God, and working. I'm ending with a thousand kisses, missing you so much. Raizel.

BLIMA

And Blima.

> RAIZEL *drops her letter and exits.* YOUNG SALA *grabs it just in time. Men and women are rounded up and marched off.* HARRY *and* YOUNG SALA *are separated. The lights change.*

DYHERNFURTH CAMP, GERMANY. MARCH 1, 1943.

> HARRY *writes a letter from his new camp.*

HARRY

My dearest Salusia—I'm miserable. It's very hard for me to write, but you could write more often, couldn't you? Tell me what you need. I've been working very hard on your transfer. Salusia, my sweet girl, go on being strong and believe in our love. I'm running out of paper, so I'll close now. Kissing you a thousand times. Harry.

SCHATZLAR LABOR CAMP, CZECHOSLOVAKIA. MARCH 5, 1944.

> NAZIS *cross the stage. We are in a new camp.* ZUSI, GUCIA, *and* RACHEL, *three new friends, enter.* ZUSI *puts them into a mock lineup.*

ZUSI

Hallo! Hallo! Occupants of Camp Number Twenty! Did you hear today's announcement? Salusia Garncarz is having her twentieth birthday. Turning twenty in Camp Number Twenty! Congratulations, Sala!

GUCIA

Sala! Quick! We've made birthday cards for you.

RACHEL
    (Looking over her shoulder.)
Careful.

GUCIA

Hurry.

YOUNG SALA

Where did you get paper?

RACHEL

Shhhh.

ZUSI
    (Quickly reading from a piece of paper.)
March fifth is a happy and a lucky day for us . . .

GUCIA
    (Quickly reading.)
Today we're celebrating our dear Sala's twentieth birthday, sadly, still behind barbed wire.

RACHEL

Did you hear something?
    They all listen.

GUCIA

Nothing. But hurry.

ZUSI

Let happiness shine on you. Let evil pass you by. Let there be hope in your heart.

RACHEL

(Quickly reading.)
Oh, what a great holiday this would be if we celebrated your birthday in freedom, together with your loved ones . . .

GUCIA

(Quickly reading.)
May you and your Harry never know adversity again.

RACHEL

(Reading even more quickly.)
May your next birthday be celebrated with your loved ones, in joy and freedom. From your friends. Rachel!

GUCIA

Gucia!

ZUSI

Zusi!

They hear a GUARD.

GUARD

Was machen sie? [What are you doing?]

ZUSI, GUCIA *and* RACHEL *drop their pieces of paper and run off.* SALA *quickly picks up the cards, as the* GUARD *approaches.*
Du Komm mit mir! [You. Come with me!]

The GUARD *grabs* SALA *roughly and begins to march her off-stage.* YOUNG SALA *holds up one of the birthday cards, but not so he can see what it is.*

YOUNG SALA

I have a pass.

The GUARD *releases her and exits.*

LATE AT NIGHT IN NEW YORK CITY, 2004

> ANN *is at the table, working, possibly in her pajamas.* SALA *enters, in her nightgown and robe.*

SALA

Go to bed.

ANN

The girls are still out.

SALA

—I'll wait for them. You've been staying up too late.

ANN

I can't sleep. It's like this door to the past, a time warp has opened. I've been given the key to the past.

SALA

It's the present that matters.

ANN

Listen to this letter. From Ala.
(*Reading.*)
"I'm proud of you and always will be and however you go on with your life, always think of me and go through life in a way that would make me . . ."

SALA

Don't cry. Don't, honey. Don't. That was a long time ago.

ANN

(*Trying not to cry.*)
Ala was proud of you.

SALA

I know she was.

ANN

You wouldn't be here today if it weren't for Ala.

SALA

Maybe not.
(*A pause.*)

ANN

Do you know what happened to Ala?

(A pause.)

SALA

Of course.

ANN

You do?

SALA

Ala died.

ANN

I've discovered something. In my research. Do you know how she died?

SALA

Everybody died.

ANN

Mommy, I need to tell you what happened to Ala.

ELISABETH *and* CAROLINE *come in, laughing.*

ELISABETH

Here we are!

CAROLINE

We're home!

ANN

It's after midnight.

CAROLINE

(To ELISABETH.*)*
I told you she'd be mad.

ANN

I'm trying to talk to your grandmother about Ala.

CAROLINE

(To ANN.*)*
She doesn't want to remember things. You're mean to her.

ELISABETH

(To CAROLINE.*)*
You've got glitter in your hair.

ELISABETH *starts to pick glitter out of* CAROLINE's *hair.* SALA
stares at them.

SALA

This reminds me of when I was in the war and every day we used to sit down at night and pick the lice out of our hair because we didn't want to lose all our hair when the war was over.

Silence.

ELISABETH

Maybe Mom's right.

CAROLINE

What?

ELISABETH

We should give the letters to the library. Then she'd have to stop.

CAROLINE

We can't give away Bubbe's letters.

ELISABETH

They're making Bubbe miserable. *(To* ANN.*)* Do it. Give the letters to the Library.

CAROLINE

(To ELISABETH.*)*
What? What do you mean?

ELISABETH

(To CAROLINE.*)*
If you cared about Bubbe you'd let her get rid of the letters.

CAROLINE

(To ELISABETH.*)*
I love Bubbe. More than you do.

ELISABETH

That's not true.

CAROLINE

You're going to give away Bubbe's letters, too. You're on her side?

(She points to ANN.*)*

ELISABETH

(To CAROLINE.*)*
There's no sides. It's about what's best for Bubbe.

ANN

Stop it. Stop it.

SALA

This isn't worth it, Annie.

ANN *and* SALA *pause, but do not freeze. Lights up on* ALA.

ALA

Dearest Sarenka—I'm here at the post office. The mail's going out today and how could I not write to my Sarenka? Bernhard and I are well and we're planning to go to the camp. Today's a gorgeous day, we're in the best of spirits and have great hopes for the future. Don't worry, everything will be fine. Be brave. Ala.

Lights fade on ALA. *Perhaps time has passed in New York.*

SALA

(To ANN.*)*
Tell me about Ala.

CAROLINE

What?

SALA

Go ahead. Tell me about Ala.

ELISABETH

Bubbe, you're upset. You should go to bed. You should be in bed.

SALA

Ala.

CAROLINE

What're you talking about?

ELISABETH

Go to bed, Bubbe.

SALA

(To ANN.*)*
What did you find out?

ANN

We can talk tomorrow.

SALA

Tell me now.

ANN

It's really late.

SALA

What happened to Ala?

ANN

Let's all go to bed.

ELISABETH

Go to bed, Bubbe.

CAROLINE

 (Overlapping.)
Let's go to bed.

SALA

How did Ala die?

ANN

I can tell you tomorrow.

SALA

You can tell me now.

 (A pause.)

ANN

Okay.

 (A beat.)

I received the confirmation today. Ala worked in the munitions factory. At Auschwitz.

ELISABETH

Don't.

SALA

What else?

ANN

It's all here. The women prisoners were smuggling out gunpowder. Tiny amounts of it, giving it to the men, to build a bomb.

CAROLINE

Bubbe, let's go to bed.

SALA

(To ANN.*)*
What else?

ANN

The women hid the gunpowder. Under their fingernails, in their underwear, their scarves, the hems of their clothing. A teaspoon a day of gunpowder. They blew up a crematorium. I can't believe it. They blew it up! They were caught.

SALA

Ala was too smart to get caught. Ala was smart.

ANN

Ala was important. She helped blow up a crematorium!

CAROLINE

Mom, stop it. It doesn't matter.

ELISABETH

No. It does matter.

ANN

Yes. Ala was important. And we have letters from her. Probably the only letters in existence with her handwriting. And we have her photo. These are the only records of Ala Gertner.

CAROLINE

So what?

ANN

You can't say no anymore. This changes everything. It's all documented. There were four women hanged at Auschwitz. For conspiracy. Ala was one of them. Ala was hanged at Auschwitz.

> GUCIA, ZUSI, *and* RACHEL *enter furtively.* GUCIA *has two pieces of paper, each with a hand-drawn colored image of a lit candle. The "wicks" are folded down.* RACHEL *carries a piece of cloth and* ZUSI *has some bread.*

GUCIA

It's almost sundown.

RACHEL

Quick!

GUCIA

Hurry up, Sala.

    YOUNG SALA *rushes in. They all crouch on the floor.*

It's Sala's turn.

YOUNG SALA

Did you find some bread?

ZUSI

Yes.

RACHEL

Shhh.

YOUNG SALA

Cover the bread.

ZUSI

I thought today was Thursday.

GUCIA

It's Friday.

RACHEL

Shhh.

ZUSI

Are you sure?

RACHEL

Hurry.

GUCIA

Hurry, Sala.

YOUNG SALA

We need candles.

GUCIA

    Holding out her pieces of paper.

Here.

ZUSI

No candles? No matches?

GUCIA

It's all I could think of.

ZUSI

I found bread.

GUCIA

I'm sorry.

RACHEL

Hush.

YOUNG SALA

It's fine. Where's the loaf of bread?

ZUSI

Holding out her hand.
It's only some crumbs.

GUCIA

That's not a loaf.

ZUSI

It's all I could find.

RACHEL

Shhh. Hurry.

YOUNG SALA

The two candles represent the commandments to remember and to keep the Sabbath. We will now light the Sabbath candles.

> GUCIA *"lights" the candles by unfolding the pieces of paper and revealing the colored flame on each.* YOUNG SALA *waves her hands over the paper candles. Then she covers her eyes and very softly recites or sings a blessing, perhaps the following:*

Blessed are you, Lord, our God, sovereign of the universe. Who has sanctified us with His commandments and commanded us to light the lights of Shabbat.

> YOUNG SALA *looks at the paper candles and then at* GUCIA.

ZUSI

Blow out the candles.

> GUCIA *folds down the pieces of paper, thus extinguishing the "candles."*

A loud whistle! GUARDS *enter, lining up the four women along with several others.*

GUARD

Stellt euch auf! [Line up!] Seh an mir! [Look at me!]

Once again, the women are in a line-up. The NAZI OFFICER *walks up and down the line, stopping in front of one woman. He points at one of the women (not* YOUNG SALA *nor her three friends.)*

OFFICER

Du. [You]

He moves on and then stops in front of YOUNG SALA *for a moment.*

GUARD

Dieser Ein? [This one?]

OFFICER

Nein. [No.]

He points to another woman.

Und du. [And you.]

WOMAN

No! No!

The GUARDS *grab the two women indicated. They are carried off, screaming.*

GUARD

(As they take the women offstage.)

Halt die Klappe! [Shut your mouth!]

There are sounds of beating heard offstage, perhaps a single gunshot. Screams, then silence. The women onstage disperse and hide.

YOUNG SALA *stands alone. She takes a piece of paper from her bosom and holds it out, as if trying to send it to* HARRY.

YOUNG SALA

Come, Harry, come to me, please. I'm so scared. I'm writing you even though I don't know where to mail the letter. Do you still think of your sweet Salusia—or is she already gone from your mind? Oh, Harry, I ask you, tell me, when will all of this end? When, when?

YOUNG SALA *continues to hold out her hand as if trying to send the letter, but no one is there to take it. She looks at it, decides to keep it herself, as there is nothing else to do. She hides the paper again in her bosom and looks back toward the Sosnowiec area, hopefully. No one is there.* YOUNG SALA *curls up and sleeps, dreaming.*

RACHEL *creeps back in and sees that* YOUNG SALA *is asleep. She holds out a card with a colored drawing on it.*

RACHEL

Sala, sometimes, when all of us are in the bunk, and you're asleep, we hear you call in your sleep: "Mommy, Daddy . . ." We don't know whether to wake you or not, because we know that, right then, at that moment, you're happy and dreaming you're with your family. Forgive us, if we sometimes disturb your sweet dreams. Happy Birthday, from Rachel.

RACHEL *leaves the card beside* YOUNG SALA *and exits.* YOUNG SALA *sleeps.*

Perhaps the older SALA *watches from the other side of the stage. Or perhaps she, too, is dreaming, sitting in a chair with her feet up. Perhaps* ANN *has her head down on her desk and is dreaming, too.*

In YOUNG SALA's *dream there is a flurry of letters being handed off to* YOUNG SALA, *as the other characters walk into and around the space, faster and faster.* YOUNG SALA *scurries to gather the letters, hiding them as fast as she can.*

VOICE [ALA]

We all hope that God will not forsake us.

VOICE [BELA]

Dear Sala—I heard that you are able to obtain great favors.

VOICE [FRYMKA]

Dear Sala—My brother Moishe was taken away today. Perhaps he's at your camp. Will you look for him?

VOICE [CHANA]

Write to us.

VOICE [GLIKA]

Be careful with your work. Be careful with the machines.

VOICE [BELA]

Please be so kind as to do my brother's laundry.

VOICE [ALA]

One must not lose faith.

VOICE [FRYMKA]

We don't know what happened to our parents.

VOICE [SARA]

My brother is at your camp. Ask him if he needs shoes.

VOICE [RAIZEL]

Sala, where is Chaim? Are you still getting mail from him?

VOICE [GLIKA]

My sister from Krakow and her child aren't here any longer; her husband committed suicide.

VOICE [ALA]

Write to us.

VOICE [SARA]

Are you getting mail from home? We don't understand why no one is writing us.

VOICE [ALA]

If you don't write, everything is lost.

The voices and the letters come faster and faster, overlapping.

VOICE [CHANA]

Have you had any news?

VOICE [SARA]

Who do you hear from?

VOICE [FRYMKA]

We have no news of Jacob.

VOICE [GLIKA]

We're very worried.

VOICE [CHANA]

Everyone has been ordered to go.

VOICE [BELA]

We have nothing to eat.

VOICE [FRYMKA]

It's unbearable.

Letters begin falling from the sky. YOUNG SALA *can no longer pick them all up.*

The voices speak faster and more insistently.

VOICE [GLIKA]

Write to us!

VOICE [SARA]

Write to us!

VOICE [FRYMKA]

Write to us!

VOICE [BLIMA]

Write to us!

VOICE [BELA]

Write to us!

VOICE [CHANA]

Write to us!

VOICE [GLIKA]

Write to us!

VOICE [SARA]

Write to us!

VOICE [FRYMKA]

Write to us!

VOICE [BLIMA]

Write to us!

VOICE [BELA]

Write to us!

VOICE [CHANA]

Write to us!

(*A beat.*)

VOICE [ALA]

If you don't write, everything is lost.

During the previous, the actresses have been exiting until the mail delivery suddenly stops.

Pieces of paper continue to fall from the sky. ZUSI, GUCIA, *and* RACHEL *enter, excitedly. The lines overlap.*

ZUSI

Look! Look! Look!

GUCIA

They're everywhere!

YOUNG SALA

What is it?

RACHEL

Don't touch them. Don't pick them up.

ZUSI

Pointing.
There's the plane.

RACHEL

Are they going to bomb us?

YOUNG SALA

Where's the plane?

GUCIA

Whose plane is it?

ZUSI

It's in the clouds. I can't see.

YOUNG SALA

What do the papers say?

RACHEL

Don't touch them.

GUCIA

Maybe the war is over.

RACHEL

Maybe it's a trap.

YOUNG SALA

How will we know?

RACHEL

Don't pick it up.

GUCIA

I can almost read it.

ZUSI

Do you think it's—

RACHEL

Is that a guard coming?
They all freeze.

YOUNG SALA

I don't hear anything.

GUCIA

I don't hear—

YOUNG SALA

I don't hear anything. It's completely quiet.
A pause, while they listen.

GUCIA

It's too quiet.

YOUNG SALA

It's never been this quiet.

ZUSI

I'm going to pick one up.

RACHEL

Don't pick it up. Just look at it. Don't touch it.

                              YOUNG SALA
I'll watch out for the guard.

                                 GUCIA
No. No! It is!

                                  ZUSI
My god. My god!

                              YOUNG SALA
          (Leaning over to read one herself.)
What?

                                 RACHEL
What?

                                 GUCIA
It's over.

          They pick up some of the leaflets and read them.

                                  ZUSI
          (Reading.)
Liberation.

                              YOUNG SALA
What?

                                  ZUSI
The war is over. That's what it says.

                                 GUCIA
Germany has surrendered.

          RACHEL *begins crying hysterically.*

                                  ZUSI
Germany has surrendered!

                              YOUNG SALA
It's over?

                                 GUCIA
It's over! It's over!

                              YOUNG SALA
Can we believe it?

A very young and hatless NAZI GUARD *suddenly runs onstage. As he races past them he tears off his jacket, drops it on the floor and races off.* RACHEL *continues to cry. The others yell toward offstage, announcing the news.*

GUCIA

The war is over!

ZUSI

(Overlapping.)
The war is over!

YOUNG SALA

(Overlapping.)
The war is over!

RACHEL

(Overlapping, still crying.)
The war is over!

GUCIA

(Overlapping.)
It's over!

ZUSI

(Overlapping.)
The war is over!

GUCIA *and* ZUSI *grab* RACHEL *and gleefully run offstage, laughing and crying. We hear them relaying the news offstage.*

YOUNG SALA *retrieves her packet of letters and looks to* SALA.

YOUNG SALA

What do we do now?

Lights fade on YOUNG SALA *as they come up on* SALA *and her granddaughters.* CAROLINE *and* ELISABETH *sit and listen, enraptured by* SALA'S *story.*

SALA

We were liberated by the Russians. I went back to my city to Poland, with a couple of my friends. Maybe somebody else from my family would be there. Where else could I go? But then something happened and I knew I wasn't going to stay in Poland. They threw me off from the trolley because I, because we didn't have any money. I was talking a perfect Polish but they didn't care . . . I said I was raised in here, born in here, went to school in here and we don't have any money, just coming straight from camp. And—I don't want to use the language, what they called me—they said get off. Get off the trolley. I never even went to my apartment, where we lived, which was why I went back in the first place. I stayed just long enough to register—There was already like a little Jewish community come back—and I registered in case someone else in the family is alive. And there was nobody in our family registered at the time. So I went on. Just went on. Everybody was looking. Asking. Do you know this one or that one. Do you know if they are alive. I couldn't find my family, so I went to Prague. I was trying to get in touch with the . . . friend . . . because he was Czechoslovakian.

CAROLINE

Harry?

SALA

And then I kept going until I was in the American zone.

CAROLINE

What happened to Harry?

SALA

You want to know? Here. I kept the telegram.

CAROLINE

That wasn't in the box.

SALA

You don't know everything.

    SALA *hands the telegram to* CAROLINE.

CAROLINE

What does it say?

SALA

    (Reciting from memory.)
"Prague. July 26, 1945. I am alive. Wait for letter. Harry."

CAROLINE

What happened?

SALA

Harry hadn't heard from me in two years. He thought I was dead.

ELISABETH

You saw him.

SALA

He sent a man. A relative. I don't know. Sent to say Harry was no longer interested. That I should leave Prague.

CAROLINE

You never saw Harry again?

SALA

No.

ELISABETH

He survived, married, and had children. Mom suspects he had a woman in every camp.

CAROLINE

Elisabeth!

ELISABETH

Mom's research!

CAROLINE
    (*To* SALA.)
Did you know that about him?

SALA

I was very young.

CAROLINE
    (*To* SALA.)
You kept the telegram. It wasn't with the letters.
    (*A beat.*)

ELISABETH
    (*To* SALA.)
You didn't try to find him in Czechoslovakia? To talk to him in person?

SALA

For what? God had other plans.

ELISABETH

If Harry had seen you in Prague—

CAROLINE

Then she wouldn't have married Poppy.

SALA

I just kept going. Looking for lists, wherever I could find them. Looking for names of people still alive. Looking for my family.

ANSBACH, GERMANY. SEPTEMBER 7, 1945.

Outside the synagogue, SIDNEY, *an American GI in uniform, approaches* YOUNG SALA.

SIDNEY

Good Yontif.

YOUNG SALA

Good Yontif.

SIDNEY

I saw you at the synagogue.

YOUNG SALA

Yes.

SIDNEY

Was it . . . strange?

YOUNG SALA

Strange?

SIDNEY

My Yiddish isn't very good.

YOUNG SALA

I don't know what language to speak anymore.

SIDNEY

I'm an American.

YOUNG SALA
Pointing to some insignia on his uniform.
Yes, I know.

SIDNEY

I'm happy to be here.

YOUNG SALA

At the synagogue?

SIDNEY

In Ansbach. In Germany. In Europe. To help.

YOUNG SALA

Thank you.

SIDNEY

No, no, no, no, no. You don't have to—I wasn't asking for—My name is
Sidney. Sidney Kirschner.

YOUNG SALA

I'm Sala Garncarz.

(*A beat.*)

SIDNEY

The synagogue is very beautiful.

YOUNG SALA

Yes, it is.

SIDNEY

Is this the first time you . . .?

YOUNG SALA

In over five years. My first service in a synagogue in over five years.

SIDNEY

I'm glad they're holding services again. It's a fine thing. The synagogue
open again. It's one of the only ones standing. Anywhere in Germany. The
mayor, as I understand it, as the locals tell it, fought to keep it. Wouldn't
let them burn it. Said the streets around it were too narrow. Said that a fire
would destroy the whole section. So they left it. We, my base, the Jewish
chaplain, actually, and some volunteers, renovated it. It's very exciting to
see it open again, having services again after so long.

YOUNG SALA

We held our own services.

A pause. SIDNEY *waits for her to speak again, but she doesn't.*

SIDNEY

It's a fine building.

YOUNG SALA *doesn't speak.*

Isn't it? A fine building?

YOUNG SALA *doesn't speak.*

Is there anything you need?

YOUNG SALA

I'm fine, thank you.

She starts to leave.

Good Yontif.

SIDNEY

May I see you again?

YOUNG SALA *walks to another area of the stage, into a spot-light.*

YOUNG SALA

(Reciting a letter.)

To the mother of Sidney Kirschner. If I could only find the proper words to the mother of such a fine American soldier. Who would imagine I would meet such a man? Your son and I want the same thing, but I won't say yes, until we get your blessing and acceptance. I wasn't given the happiness of being able to ask my dearest mother for her blessing. It's possible that my family would have said the same as you, that Sidney and I don't really know each other. But I can tell you I'm a plain Jewish girl from a kosher home and that's all. I think it's enough. Sala.

Lights fade on YOUNG SALA.

NEW YORK CITY, 2004

ANN *and* SALA *are returning from* RAIZEL's *funeral, with* CAROLINE *and* ELISABETH. SALA *sees* RAIZEL *on the other side of the stage.* RAIZEL, *now a ghost as well as a memory, walks purposefully into the New York City living room. Only* SALA *can see her.*

RAIZEL

(The letter pours out from her; she barely pauses for a breath.)

Dearest newly found little sister, we got your letter today. My hands are trembling. I don't know where to begin.

SALA *is aware of the others and interacts with them when necessary, but her focus is on* RAIZEL.

ANN

Mother, wasn't that a lovely service?

CAROLINE

I didn't understand a single word.

ANN

Aunt Rose would have loved all the Yiddish.

RAIZEL

(To SALA.*)*

I'm writing you in Yiddish to honor our parents.

ELISABETH

Bubbe, do you need anything?

CAROLINE

I didn't think there would be so many people.

ANN

Mother, wasn't it lovely that so many of Aunt Rose's old students were there for her funeral?

RAIZEL

(To SALA.*)*

Sala, I thought Blima and I had nobody left.

ELISABETH

Sit down, Bubbe.

RAIZEL

Nobody.

CAROLINE

When did she change her name from Raizel to Rose?

ANN

Before you were born, I guess.

CAROLINE

Will it say Rose or Raizel on her tombstone in Israel?

ANN

The school must have gotten the word out. And here I didn't think there were that many people left who knew Aunt Rose.

RAIZEL

(*To* SALA.)

And now to hear that you're alive! And engaged! I don't know what to say. Is he Jewish?

ANN

Standing room only. Mother, you must be exhausted.

ELISABETH

Bubbe, do you want some water?

RAIZEL

(*To* SALA.)

How happy our dear parents would have been, had they lived. To lead you, the youngest child, to the wedding canopy.

CAROLINE

Now we have to keep all of Aunt Rose's letters.

ANN

You know that's not the agreement.

CAROLINE

We have to keep some of them.

ANN

Ten. We get to keep ten. That's the new deal with the library.

RAIZEL

(*To* SALA.)

Have you found anyone else from our family?

CAROLINE

How can we choose?

ANN

If you don't choose, I'll choose for you. Ala's letters should all go to the library. She's an historical figure. You could pick the more personal letters.

CAROLINE

They're all personal. Bubbe's not historical.

The women go through the letters while SALA *watches* RAIZEL.

RAIZEL

(*To* SALA.)

My dearest Sala, may you never, never again know suffering.

ELISABETH

This is really hard.

ANN

Maybe now you're beginning to understand how responsible I've felt.

CAROLINE

You were given the letters because you were next in line. You're the daughter. And we're in line after you.

ANN

I'm protecting—

ELISABETH

Are we starting this again? Today?

CAROLINE

(*To* ANN.)

It's selfish. You're selfish.

ANN

I'm not—

CAROLINE

Selfish.

ANN

No.

CAROLINE

You are.

ELISABETH

Mom, you've always acted like the letters were just yours.

ANN

I walked out of the first New York Public Library agreement because you both asked me to. And when we found out about Ala I made a completely new deal. I did that for you. I was hoping we could finally move past all this disagreement.

RAIZEL

(To SALA.*)*

We only want to be together again. Let's not lose hope.

ANN

We're keeping ten letters for the family. And you can see the rest at the library. Those big stone lions will be guarding the letters.

CAROLINE

So we go with our family to a cold room, watched by a security guard as we relive our history?

ANN

Yes. Anytime you want.

CAROLINE

Can we see the letters in the middle of the night? What if Bubbe wants to see them in the middle of the night?

ELISABETH

Mom, they're not going to open the library in the middle of the night.

ANN

Yes, that would be pretty selfish to ask for.

CAROLINE

You're selfish. You're unfeeling. You're a terrible mother.

ANN

I'm sorry you feel that way.

CAROLINE

How can you do this to us? How can you do this to Bubbe? And to Aunt Rose?

ANN

Aunt Rose didn't want to talk about it.

RAIZEL

(To SALA.*)*

No matter how much I write, it could not, would not measure up to the reality of it all.

ANN

And Bubbe didn't want the letters anymore. I wish you could understand.

ELISABETH

I wish you could both understand.

ANN

Here's what I understand. Your Aunt Raizel survived a death march. Over two months. Twenty, thirty miles a day. And after that Bergen Belsen. She survived a death march AND a death camp!

RAIZEL

(*To* SALA.)

Finally, after all our sufferings, after six years of horror and separation, Blima and I will be able to hug you tight, close to our hearts. Longing for you, Raizel.

RAIZEL *and* SALA *sit together, in silence.*

CAROLINE

Bubbe, what do you think?

ELISABETH

Bubbe's too nice to say anything.

CAROLINE

(*To* ANN.)

I can't believe you're her daughter.

ANN

I certainly am her daughter. Your grandmother saved the letters and now I'm saving them, too. If you don't choose which letters to keep, I'm going to do it for you.

ELISABETH

That's not fair. Caroline hasn't even read them all.

CAROLINE

I have, too. I've read a translation of every single letter.

ANN

Good. Read this one. It's the poem she wrote for New Year's.

CAROLINE

I've read it.

ANN

Read it again. Read it out loud.

CAROLINE

Now?

ANN

Now. And tomorrow. And the next day. Read it every day.

CAROLINE
(*Defiantly reading.*)
"Yet again, we spend our most solemn holiday behind bars.
In the future, it'll be hard to believe that we waited so long for our freedom."

CAROLINE *pauses, choking up.*

ANN

Keep reading.

CAROLINE
(*Struggling to read.*)
"We can't understand
How we were caught in this terrible trap."

CAROLINE *stops reading.* ANN *takes the poem from her.*

ANN
(*Reading.*)
"Spending years away from home, in the most miserable conditions
Busy only with work, and contemplating the horrors around us.
This is the most severe blow they dealt."

On the other side of the stage, YOUNG SALA *is reading the same poem.*

ANN, YOUNG SALA
(*Reading.*)
"However, we are quite strong.
We will tell ourselves to endure.
After all,
Jews are used to it."

ANN

You want to keep that in a box?

CAROLINE *begins to cry.*

Read it.

CAROLINE

I can't.

ANN

Read the end.

CAROLINE

I don't want to.

ANN

Read it. And don't ever forget it.

ELISABETH *takes the paper from* CAROLINE. ELISABETH *and* ANN *speak the poem together,* ELISABETH *reading and* ANN *reciting it from memory,* YOUNG SALA *reading on the other side of the stage.*

ELISABETH & YOUNG SALA

(Reading.)
"Let us hope, and let us be confident,
That soon we'll be one with our parents, and with our family.
This is the essence of our prayer."

ANN

(To CAROLINE.*)*
Do you want to put that back in a box? Or do you want to share it with the world?

ANN *takes the letters that are out on the table and quickly puts them in the box, one by one, while she reads the name of each sender.*

Sara Czarka. Rozia Grunbaum. Raizel Garncarz. Laya Dina. Ala Gertner. Chaim Kaufman. Raizel. Blima. Zusi Ginter. Raizel. Raizel. Gucia Gutman. Bela Kohn. Ala Gertner. Do you want to keep all these people in a box for no one to ever know about? Frymka Rabinowicz. Sara Rabinowicz. Moshe David. Ala Gertner. Ala. Ala. Ala . . . There. They're in the box. Is that what you want?

CAROLINE

I don't know.

ANN

Here. Take it.

ANN *pushes the box toward* CAROLINE, *who is in tears.* ANN *turns away.*

SALA

Caroline. Elisabeth.

They look at her.

There was a time where I wanted to not be Jewish anymore. But then I said, but my parents died because of it, how can I betray them and not be Jewish anymore? Sometimes I was very angry, especially when I was away in camps. Still get angry sometimes, very angry. I came out; I had nobody. Nobody around, no family. We would be maybe a hundred people now from all the sisters and brothers and we're not. And that makes you angry, right? Why? Why? Why? There's no answer. But I have faith. I don't know what it is, but I'm holding onto it.

CAROLINE *picks up the box. She exchanges a look with* ELISABETH.

ELISABETH

Mom?

ANN

What?

ELISABETH

(Confirming.)
We can each keep one letter?

ANN

Yes.

CAROLINE

Glancing again at ELISABETH.
Okay. I'm going to keep one of Aunt Raizel's letters.

CAROLINE *hands the box to* ANN. ELISABETH *and* CAROLINE *hug each other.*

RAIZEL

(Reciting a letter.)
It's twelve o'clock now on Friday. In my imagination I see our dear mother fussing in the kitchen, preparing for Shabbat. Our father, too.

CAROLINE & RAIZEL
(CAROLINE is reading from the letter as RAIZEL recites.)
"Sala, I see our father again, his voice comes to me day and night."

ELISABETH
(Reading from another letter.)
"I read every one of your letters to him ten times. You can't imagine what they meant to him."

CAROLINE
(Reading from a different letter.)
"Our dear parents, they gave us their future."

ANN
(Reading from another letter.)
"We have nobody left. Nobody!"

RAIZEL
I wish I had a picture, so that I could at least kiss Poppa's high forehead and his long grey beard.

ANN, YOUNG SALA
(Reading.)
"I have the pictures!"

YOUNG SALA
I have the pictures of our dear father and dear mother, together with all the mail I received from home, starting from the first minute that I left for camp.

CAROLINE *notices* YOUNG SALA *on the other side of the stage, looking at her.*

SALA/YOUNG SALA
(Together/Reading/Reciting.)
"All along, I watched it and guarded it like the eyes in my head, since it was my greatest treasure."

ELISABETH *sees* YOUNG SALA. *There is a recognition.*

SALA
(Reading.)
"It was my greatest treasure."

YOUNG SALA

(Reading.)
"I have all the mail I received from home."

ANN

(Reading.)
"I have all the mail."

ELISABETH *and* CAROLINE *continue to look at* YOUNG SALA.

SALA

(Reading.)
"I have all the mail I received from home, starting from the first minute
that I left for camp. Because if I lost them these people would die. I keep
them alive by saving the letters."

> YOUNG SALA *walks toward the New York scene, stopping just
> shy of that playing area. Only* CAROLINE *and* ELISABETH *see her.*

> SALA *and* ANN *continue to look at the letters.* CAROLINE *and*
> ELISABETH *walk toward* YOUNG SALA, *The three meet cen-
> ter stage and stand looking at each other.* YOUNG SALA *holds
> her packet of letters toward* CAROLINE *and* ELISABETH. *Just
> before they have a chance to reach out for the letters, the lights
> fade to black.*

Or:

> ELISABETH *and* CAROLINE *keep looking at the letters with*
> ANN *while* SALA *and* YOUNG SALA *share a last moment as the
> lights fade to black.*

> *Then, before the curtain call, the audience should see or hear
> the following, either on a projection screen or spoken by the
> actors playing the roles. There may be photos of the letters and
> real people shown on a projection screen.*

ONE OF THE ENSEMBLE WOMEN ACTORS

From 1940 to 1946 Sala Garncarz collected 352 letters, documents, and photographs, currently preserved as the Sala Garncarz Kirschner Collection at the New York Public Library.

The screen changes to photos of CHANA *and* JOSEPH.

THE ACTOR PLAYING CHANA

Sala's parents died at Auschwitz.

The screen changes to photos of RAIZEL *and* BLIMA.

THE ACTOR PLAYING RAIZEL

Raizel and Blima survived the death march from Neusalz.

THE ACTOR PLAYING BLIMA

Both married, but had no children.

The screen changes to the photo of HARRY *and* SALA.

THE ACTOR PLAYING HARRY

Harry Haubenstock survived the war, married, and had two daughters.

The screen changes to the photo of ELFRIEDE.

THE ACTOR PLAYING ELFRIEDE

Elfriede Pache married and had two children.

The screen changes to the photo of ALA.

THE ACTOR PLAYING ALA

In 1991 Ala Gertner was one of the four women recognized with the memorial at Yad Vashem in Jerusalem.

The screen changes to the photo of SALA *and* SIDNEY *in uniform.*

THE ACTOR PLAYING ELISABETH

Sala Garncarz married Sidney Kirschner.

THE ACTOR PLAYING CAROLINE

They had three children, eight grandchildren, and eight great-grandchildren.

> *The screen changes to a photo of* SALA *and* SIDNEY *in their 80s.*

THE ACTOR PLAYING ANN

Sala and Sidney celebrated their seventy-second wedding anniversary in March 2018.
[Note: change the date for each production as needed. Sala was married on March 5, 1946, in Germany; on June 8, 1946, in New York City.]

> *[Please check the website for updates to this information, including details about other family members.]*

> *The screen changes to the flyer for the New York Public Library exhibition or the book jacket for Sala's Gift by Ann Kirschner.*

END OF PLAY.

Pronuncation Guide

Sala	SAH-la
Garncarz	GARN-sah-sh
Raizel	RYE-zull
Chana	*(guttural)* CKHAH-na / HAH-nah
Blima	BLEE-ma
Sarenka	Sah-RAIN-ko
Ala	AH-la
Gertner	*(hard G)* GAIRT-ner
Salusia	Sah-LOO-she-ya
Lucia	LOO-sha
Rozia	ROUGE-ya
Frymka	FRIM-kuh
Haubenstock	HOW-ben-stock
Elfriede	El-FREE-duh
Chaim	*(guttural)* CKH-EYE-eem or HI-eem
Pache	*(guttural, like "Bach")* or POCK-a
Laya Dina	LAY-ah DEE-nah
Gucia	GOOOD-cha
Zusi	ZOO-see
Glika	GLEE-kuh
Sosnowiec	So-SNO vee-yetz
Geppersdorf	*(hard G)* GEP-pers-dorf
Neusalz	NOY-salts

Acknowledgments

It's impossible to express my gratitude to Ann Kirschner, an extraordinary woman, who has been inspiring, kind, encouraging, and helpful through every stage of the writing process and beyond, even when I made her into a sometimes unsympathetic character in the play. Ann has been tireless in her support, traveling to college productions during early works-in-progress, helping fundraise for development opportunities, and continuing to visit online with student casts and their teachers/directors around the country.

And I have to thank Tracy Carns, the best of editors, for her patience, persistence, expertise, and friendship.

Special thanks: Margot Avery, Seth Barrish, Lee Brock, Amanda Card, James Carlson, Jennifer Cavanaugh, Suz Claassen, Lynn Cohen, Patrick Flick, Julie Gagnes, Elizabeth Grammer, Roger Hall, Alice Jankell, Blair Johnson, Sala Garncarz Kirschner, Sidney Kirschner, Konnie Kittrell, David Landon, Laura Lippman, Mark Lutwak, Michael Mah, Janine McCabe, Pat McLaughlin, Bob McNamara, Todd McNerney, Lyndol Michael, Eric Nightengale, Ruth Nightengale, Julie Nives, Murray Nossel, Cheri Peters, Craig Pospisil, Wyatt Prunty, Michelle Sacharow, Nina Sacharow, Stephanie Sandberg, Britian Seibert, Marian Seldes, Pete Smith, Cathy Tempelsman, Patty Uffelman, Wendy Vanden Heuvel, Jill Vexler, Caroline Weinberg, Elisabeth Weinberg, John & Laura Willis.

Also to: The Addlestone Library, the Barrow Group, CATO Center Artist in Resident Endowment, the College of Charleston Department of Theatre and Dance, Ensemble Studio Theatre Playwrights Unit, FAB Women@TBG, French Children of the Holocaust Foundation, James Madison University, the Journey Company, Macaulay Honors College, the MacDowell Colony, the Museum of Jewish Heritage, New Dramatists, New York Foundation for the Arts, The Overlook Press, Rollins College, Seattle Pacific University, the Sewanee Young Writers Conference, Stagedoor Manor, the Estate of Tennessee Williams, the Corporation of Yaddo.